PRENTICE HALL

SCIENCE EXPLORER

Sound and Light

PRENTICE HALL
Needham, Massachusetts
Upper Saddle River, New Jersey

PRENTICE HALL
SCIENCE EXPLORER

Sound and Light

Program Resources

Student Edition
Annotated Teacher's Edition
Teaching Resources Book with Color Transparencies
Sound and Light Materials Kits

Program Components

Integrated Science Laboratory Manual
Integrated Science Laboratory Manual, Teacher's Edition
Inquiry Skills Activity Book
Student-Centered Science Activity Books
Program Planning Guide
Guided Reading English Audiotapes
Guided Reading Spanish Audiotapes and Summaries
Product Testing Activities by Consumer Reports™
Event-Based Science Series (NSF funded)
Prentice Hall Interdisciplinary Explorations
Cobblestone, Odyssey, Calliope, and *Faces* Magazines

Media/Technology

Science Explorer Interactive Student Tutorial CD-ROMs
Odyssey of Discovery CD-ROMs
Resource Pro® (Teaching Resources on CD-ROM)
Assessment Resources CD-ROM with Dial-A-Test®
Internet site at www.science-explorer.phschool.com
Life, Earth, and Physical Science Videodiscs
Life, Earth, and Physical Science Videotapes

Science Explorer Student Editions

From Bacteria to Plants

Animals

Cells and Heredity

Human Biology and Health

Environmental Science

Inside Earth

Earth's Changing Surface

Earth's Waters

Weather and Climate

Astronomy

Chemical Building Blocks

Chemical Interactions

Motion, Forces, and Energy

Electricity and Magnetism

Sound and Light

Staff Credits

The people who made up the *Science Explorer* team—representing editorial, editorial services, design services, field marketing, market research, marketing services, on-line services/multimedia development, product marketing, production services, and publishing processes—are listed below. Bold type denotes core team members.

Kristen E. Ball, **Barbara A. Bertell,** Peter W. Brooks, **Christopher R. Brown, Greg Cantone,** Jonathan Cheney, **Patrick Finbarr Connolly,** Loree Franz, Donald P. Gagnon, Jr., **Paul J. Gagnon, Joel Gendler,** Elizabeth Good, Kerri Hoar, **Linda D. Johnson,** Katherine M. Kotik, Russ Lappa, Marilyn Leitao, David Lippman, **Eve Melnechuk, Natania Mlawer,** Paul W. Murphy, **Cindy A. Noftle,** Julia F. Osborne, Caroline M. Power, Suzanne J. Schineller, **Susan W. Tafler,** Kira Thaler-Marbit, Robin L. Santel, Ronald Schachter, **Mark Tricca,** Diane Walsh, Pearl B. Weinstein, Beth Norman Winickoff

ISBN 0-13-434493-6
3 4 5 6 7 8 9 10   05 04 03 02 01 00 99

Cover: This French horn is shown against a background of the visible spectrum.

Program Authors

Michael J. Padilla, Ph.D.
Professor
Department of Science Education
University of Georgia
Athens, Georgia

Michael Padilla is a leader in middle school science educa-tion. He has served as an editor and elected officer for the National Science Teachers Association. He has been prin-cipal investigator of several National Science Foundation and Eisenhower grants and served as a writer of the National Science Education Standards.

As lead author of *Science Explorer,* Mike has inspired the team in developing a program that meets the needs of middle grades students, promotes science inquiry, and is aligned with the National Science Education Standards.

Ioannis Miaoulis, Ph.D.
Dean of Engineering
College of Engineering
Tufts University
Medford, Massachusetts

Martha Cyr, Ph.D.
Director, Engineering
    Educational Outreach
College of Engineering
Tufts University
Medford, Massachusetts

Science Explorer was created in collaboration with the College of Engineering at Tufts University. Tufts has an extensive engineering outreach program that uses engi-neering design and construction to excite and motivate students and teachers in science and technology education.

Faculty from Tufts University participated in the development of *Science Explorer* chapter projects, reviewed the student books for content accuracy, and helped coordinate field testing.

CHAPTER PROJECT

Book Author

Jay M. Pasachoff, Ph.D.
Professor of Astronomy
Williams College
Williamstown, Massachusetts

Contributing Writers

Rose-Marie Botting
Science Teacher
Broward County School District
Fort Lauderdale, Florida

John Coffey
Science/Mathematics Teacher
Venice Area Middle School
Venice, Florida

Edward Evans
Former Science Teacher
Hilton Central School
Hilton, New York

Peter Kahan
Former Science Teacher
Dwight-Englewood School
Englewood, New Jersey

Reading Consultant

Bonnie B. Armbruster, Ph.D.
Department of Curriculum
    and Instruction
University of Illinois
Champaign, Illinois

Interdisciplinary Consultant

Heidi Hayes Jacobs, Ed.D.
Teacher's College
Columbia University
New York, New York

Safety Consultants

W. H. Breazeale, Ph.D.
Department of Chemistry
College of Charleston
Charleston, South Carolina

Ruth Hathaway, Ph.D.
Hathaway Consulting
Cape Girardeau, Missouri

Tufts University Program Reviewers

Behrouz Abedian, Ph.D.
Department of Mechanical
Engineering

Wayne Chudyk, Ph.D.
Department of Civil and
Environmental Engineering

Eliana DeBernardez-Clark, Ph.D.
Department of Chemical Engineering

Anne Marie Desmarais, Ph.D.
Department of Civil and
Environmental Engineering

David Kaplan, Ph.D.
Department of Chemical Engineering

Paul Kelley, Ph.D.
Department of Electro-Optics

George S. Mumford, Ph.D.
Professor of Astronomy, Emeritus

Jan A. Pechenik, Ph.D.
Department of Biology

Livia Racz, Ph.D.
Department of Mechanical Engineering

Robert Rifkin, M.D.
School of Medicine

Jack Ridge, Ph.D.
Department of Geology

Chris Swan, Ph.D.
Department of Civil and
Environmental Engineering

Peter Y. Wong, Ph.D.
Department of Mechanical Engineering

Content Reviewers

Jack W. Beal, Ph.D.
Department of Physics
Fairfield University
Fairfield, Connecticut

W. Russell Blake, Ph.D.
Planetarium Director
Plymouth Community
Intermediate School
Plymouth, Massachusetts

Howard E. Buhse, Jr., Ph.D.
Department of Biological Sciences
University of Illinois
Chicago, Illinois

Dawn Smith Burgess, Ph.D.
Department of Geophysics
Stanford University
Stanford, California

A. Malcolm Campbell, Ph.D.
Assistant Professor
Davidson College
Davidson, North Carolina

Elizabeth A. De Stasio, Ph.D.
Associate Professor of Biology
Lawrence University
Appleton, Wisconsin

John M. Fowler, Ph.D.
Former Director of Special Projects
National Science Teacher's Association
Arlington, Virginia

Jonathan Gitlin, M.D.
School of Medicine
Washington University
St. Louis, Missouri

Dawn Graff-Haight, Ph.D., CHES
Department of Health, Human
Performance, and Athletics
Linfield College
McMinnville, Oregon

Deborah L. Gumucio, Ph.D.
Associate Professor
Department of Anatomy and Cell Biology
University of Michigan
Ann Arbor, Michigan

William S. Harwood, Ph.D.
Dean of University Division and Associate
Professor of Education
Indiana University
Bloomington, Indiana

Cyndy Henzel, Ph.D.
Department of Geography
and Regional Development
University of Arizona
Tucson, Arizona

Greg Hutton
Science and Health
Curriculum Coordinator
School Board of Sarasota County
Sarasota, Florida

Susan K. Jacobson, Ph.D.
Department of Wildlife Ecology
and Conservation
University of Florida
Gainesville, Florida

Judy Jernstedt, Ph. D.
Department of Agronomy and Range Science
University of California, Davis
Davis, California

John L. Kermond, Ph.D.
Office of Global Programs
National Oceanographic and
Atmospheric Administration
Silver Spring, Maryland

David E. LaHart, Ph.D.
Institute of Science and Public Affairs
Florida State University
Tallahassee, Florida

Joe Leverich, Ph.D.
Department of Biology
St. Louis University
St. Louis, Missouri

Dennis K. Lieu, Ph.D.
Department of Mechanical Engineering
University of California
Berkeley, California

Cynthia J. Moore, Ph.D.
Science Outreach Coordinator
Washington University
St. Louis, Missouri

Joseph M. Moran, Ph.D.
Department of Earth Science
University of Wisconsin–Green Bay
Green Bay, Wisconsin

Joseph Stukey, Ph.D.
Department of Biology
Hope College
Holland, Michigan

Seetha Subramanian
Lexington Community College
University of Kentucky
Lexington, Kentucky

Carl L. Thurman, Ph.D.
Department of Biology
University of Northern Iowa
Cedar Falls, Iowa

Edward D. Walton, Ph.D.
Department of Chemistry
California State Polytechnic University
Pomona, California

Robert S. Young, Ph.D.
Department of Geosciences and
Natural Resource Management
Western Carolina University
Cullowhee, North Carolina

Edward J. Zalisko, Ph.D.
Department of Biology
Blackburn College
Carlinville, Illinois

Teacher Reviewers

Stephanie Anderson
Sierra Vista Junior
    High School
Canyon Country, California

John W. Anson
Mesa Intermediate School
Palmdale, California

Pamela Arline
Lake Taylor Middle School
Norfolk, Virginia

Lynn Beason
College Station Jr. High School
College Station, Texas

Richard Bothmer
Hollis School District
Hollis, New Hampshire

Jeffrey C. Callister
Newburgh Free Academy
Newburgh, New York

Judy D'Albert
Harvard Day School
Corona Del Mar, California

Betty Scott Dean
Guilford County Schools
McLeansville, North Carolina

Sarah C. Duff
Baltimore City Public Schools
Baltimore, Maryland

Melody Law Ewey
Holmes Junior High School
Davis, California

Sherry L. Fisher
Lake Zurich Middle
    School North
Lake Zurich, Illinois

Melissa Gibbons
Fort Worth ISD
Fort Worth, Texas

Debra J. Goodding
Kraemer Middle School
Placentia, California

Jack Grande
Weber Middle School
Port Washington, New York

Steve Hills
Riverside Middle School
Grand Rapids, Michigan

Carol Ann Lionello
Kraemer Middle School
Placentia, California

Jaime A. Morales
Henry T. Gage Middle School
Huntington Park, California

Patsy Partin
Cameron Middle School
Nashville, Tennessee

Deedra H. Robinson
Newport News Public Schools
Newport News, Virginia

Bonnie Scott
Clack Middle School
Abilene, Texas

Charles M. Sears
Belzer Middle School
Indianapolis, Indiana

Barbara M. Strange
Ferndale Middle School
High Point, North Carolina

Jackie Louise Ulfig
Ford Middle School
Allen, Texas

Kathy Usina
Belzer Middle School
Indianapolis, Indiana

Heidi M. von Oetinger
L'Anse Creuse Public School
Harrison Township, Michigan

Pam Watson
Hill Country Middle School
Austin, Texas

Activity Field Testers

Nicki Bibbo
Russell Street School
Littleton, Massachusetts

Connie Boone
Fletcher Middle School
Jacksonville Beach, Florida

Rose-Marie Botting
Broward County
    School District
Fort Lauderdale, Florida

Colleen Campos
Laredo Middle School
Aurora, Colorado

Elizabeth Chait
W. L. Chenery Middle School
Belmont, Massachusetts

Holly Estes
Hale Middle School
Stow, Massachusetts

Laura Hapgood
Plymouth Community
    Intermediate School
Plymouth, Massachusetts

Sandra M. Harris
Winman Junior High School
Warwick, Rhode Island

Jason Ho
Walter Reed Middle School
Los Angeles, California

Joanne Jackson
Winman Junior High School
Warwick, Rhode Island

Mary F. Lavin
Plymouth Community
    Intermediate School
Plymouth, Massachusetts

James MacNeil, Ph.D.
Concord Public Schools
Concord, Massachusetts

Lauren Magruder
St. Michael's Country
    Day School
Newport, Rhode Island

Jeanne Maurand
Glen Urquhart School
Beverly Farms, Massachusetts

Warren Phillips
Plymouth Community
    Intermediate School
Plymouth, Massachusetts

Carol Pirtle
Hale Middle School
Stow, Massachusetts

Kathleen M. Poe
Kirby-Smith Middle School
Jacksonville, Florida

Cynthia B. Pope
Ruffner Middle School
Norfolk, Virginia

Anne Scammell
Geneva Middle School
Geneva, New York

Karen Riley Sievers
Callanan Middle School
Des Moines, Iowa

David M. Smith
Howard A. Eyer Middle School
Macungie, Pennsylvania

Derek Strohschneider
Plymouth Community
    Intermediate School
Plymouth, Massachusetts

Sallie Teames
Rosemont Middle School
Fort Worth, Texas

Gene Vitale
Parkland Middle School
McHenry, Illinois

Zenovia Young
Meyer Levin Junior
    High School (IS 285)
Brooklyn, New York

PRENTICE HALL
SCIENCE EXPLORER

Contents

Sound and Light

Activities

Turning Down the Volume on
SONIC BOOMS

Dr. Christine Mann Darden grew up in Monroe, North Carolina. She received her Ph.D. in Mechanical Engineering at George Washington University in Washington, D.C. A national expert on sonic booms, she now works at NASA's Langley Research Center in Hampton, Virginia. She manages a group of scientists who are developing supersonic airplanes. Dr. Darden (center) is shown here with other members of the Sonic Boom Group, Kathy Needleman (left) and Robert Mack (right).

*I*t happens every time a space shuttle returns to Earth. The spacecraft drops down from orbit and streaks toward its landing site in Florida or California. A few seconds after it passes overhead—BOOM! A window-rattling sound like a giant cannon shot is heard. Most scientists at the space center are monitoring the shuttle itself when it comes down from a mission. But Dr. Christine Darden is more interested in that big boom.

Dr. Darden is a research engineer at the National Aeronautics and Space Administration (NASA). She is in charge of the space agency's Sonic Boom Group. Her team of scientists is investigating the distinctive "sound print" made by aircraft that travel faster than the speed of sound. Dr. Darden and her co-workers are looking for ways to soften sonic booms. They hope to make supersonic travel—travel at speeds faster than the speed of sound—more common in the future.

Talking with Dr. Christine Darden

Breaking the Sound Barrier

The sound barrier was first broken in 1947. Since then, people have complained about sonic booms so much that the government has passed regulations. It's now against the law to fly most aircraft at supersonic speeds over the United States.

"If it is loud enough, a sonic boom can actually break windows and do damage to buildings," says Dr. Darden. "People find it very disturbing. Right now, the boom is one of the biggest obstacles to commercial supersonic air service."

Today supersonic aircraft such as the Concorde fly mainly over the ocean. But what if scientists can find ways to lower the volume of sonic booms? Then someday supersonic commercial jets may be allowed to fly across the country.

What Is a Sonic Boom?

You have probably heard the sound that is made when an airplane breaks the sound barrier. A sonic boom sounds like a clap of thunder or a sharp explosion high in the sky. Just what are you hearing?

"A sonic boom is a compression or pressure wave," Dr. Darden explains. "An airplane pushes a wave of air molecules ahead of it as it travels forward, just as a ship's bow pushes out a wave as it moves through the water. Those compressions travel outward from the plane as a shock wave of high pressure. When that shock wave reaches our ears, we hear it as a boom."

Both the SR-71 Blackbird (above) and F-16 (opposite page) are military supersonic planes.

"Think of blowing up a balloon," Dr. Darden says. "With the balloon inflated, the air on the inside is much more compressed than the air on the outside. When the balloon pops, the compression immediately flies outward in the form of a shock wave."

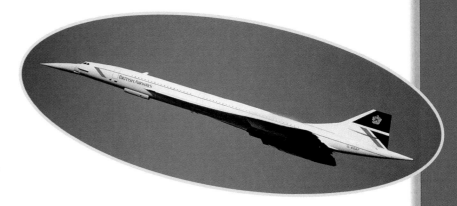

Scheduled flights of the Concorde, a supersonic commercial plane, are only made between New York and London or Paris.

How Do You Research What You Can't See?

"Part of our work is coming up with new ways to observe and measure the phenomenon we're studying," says Dr. Darden. "For example, we know that all waves have similar properties. So we look at how waves behave in water to tell us something about how they behave in the air."

Choosing Engineering

Dr. Darden's study of waves in water and air is a long way from her first career as a math teacher. In the late 1960s, she was teaching in a school in Hampton, Virginia. At that time, the NASA labs nearby were working on a program to send astronauts to the moon. Dr. Darden went to work for NASA as a mathematician.

She quickly became fascinated with the work of the NASA research engineers. "They were the ones who were working with the really tough challenges of the program," she says. "They were doing the interesting, hands-on work." As a result of her experience, she decided to get a graduate degree in engineering.

How Do You Test Supersonic Aircraft?

Working hands-on is one way that Dr. Darden and her team study how airplanes create sonic booms. They

1 A sonic boom results when an airplane moves at supersonic speed. Air is compressed at the front of the plane, creating shock waves.

2 The shock waves move out behind the plane in a cone shape.

3 When the shock waves reach the ground, people hear them as a sonic boom.

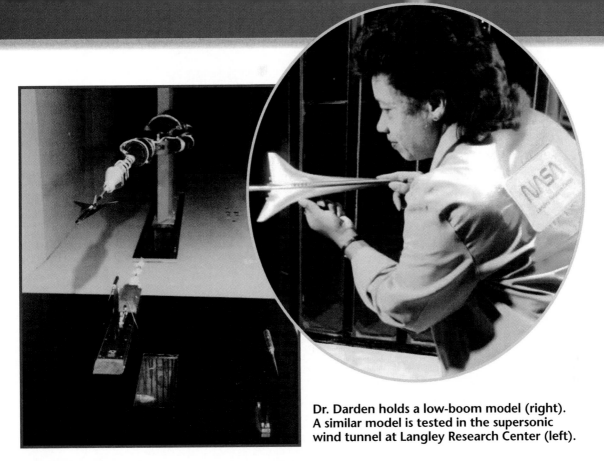

Dr. Darden holds a low-boom model (right). A similar model is tested in the supersonic wind tunnel at Langley Research Center (left).

"fly" model aircraft in a high-speed wind tunnel. The scientists place the steel models in the tunnel and watch how they behave in winds moving at up to three times the speed of sound. (The speed of sound varies with altitude and air pressure. At sea level on a 16°C day, the speed of sound is about 1,207 kilometers per hour.)

Instruments on the sides of the tunnel allow Dr. Darden to "hear" the sonic boom created by the model. By adding very fine smoke, she can even watch how the air moves over the plane. "We can actually see the shock wave," she says.

Can the Sonic Boom Effect Be Reduced?

Dr. Darden and her group at NASA have found that the shape of an aircraft determines the size of the boom it creates. They have performed tests with computer programs, on actual supersonic jets, and in wind tunnels. Their experiments have shown that angling the wings back sharply reduces the size of the shock wave and the loudness of the sonic boom. But the same features that make planes quieter also make them harder to fly.

"You could put a needle up there supersonically and you wouldn't get a sonic boom," explains Dr. Darden. "But you wouldn't have much of an airplane, either."

In Your Journal

In her research, Dr. Darden made predictions about how the angle of an airplane wing might affect a sonic boom. Then her team set up a series of experiments to test these predictions.

Now think of different-shaped boats moving through water: a kayak, a tugboat, and a rowboat. Predict the type of wave that each boat will make. How could you use models to test your predictions?

CHAPTER 1

Characteristics of Waves

WHAT'S AHEAD

 SECTION 1 **What Are Waves?**

Discover **How Do Waves Travel?**

 SECTION 2 **Properties of Waves**

Discover **How Can You Change a Wave?**
Skills Lab **Wavy Motions**

 SECTION 3 **Interactions of Waves**

Discover **How Does a Ball Bounce?**
Sharpen Your Skills **Observing**
Try This **Standing Waves**
Skills Lab **Making Waves**

12 ◆ O

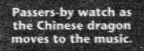

Over and Over and Over Again

It's time to celebrate the Chinese New Year! The parade passes through the streets to the delight of the people watching. The dragon dancers use poles to move the dragon up and down. The dragon moves just like a wave.

In this chapter, you will discover how waves travel. Some waves involve repeating patterns, or cycles. Any motion that repeats itself at regular intervals is called periodic motion. The hands on a clock, a child on a swing, a ride on a Ferris wheel, and your heartbeat are just a few examples of periodic motion. As you work through the project, you will investigate the properties of periodic motion.

Your Goal To find and describe examples of periodic motion.

To complete this project you will
◆ identify several examples of periodic motion or other events that have periodic characteristics
◆ collect and organize data on the frequency and duration of each event
◆ present your findings as a poster, display, or demonstration

Get Started Brainstorm examples of repeating patterns you have observed. Think about objects or events that go back and forth or alternate from high to low, dark to light, loud to quiet, or crowded to uncrowded.

Check Your Progress You'll be working on this project as you study this chapter. To keep your project on track, look for Check Your Progress boxes at the following points.
Section 1 Review, page 17: List examples of periodic motion you'd like to study.
Section 2 Review, page 23: Record your observations of the frequency, length, and amplitude of the periodic events.

Wrap Up At the end of the project (page 37), you will present your findings to your class.

Passers-by watch as the Chinese dragon moves to the music.

Integrating Earth Science

SECTION
4 **Seismic Waves**

Discover **Can You Find the Sand?**

SECTION
① What Are Waves?

How Do Waves Travel?

1. Fill a shallow pan with about 3 centimeters of water.

2. With a pencil, touch the surface of the water at one end of the pan twice each second for about a minute.

3. Describe the pattern the waves make. Sketch a rough diagram of what you see.

4. Float a cork on the water. How do you think the cork will move if there are waves? Repeat Step 2 to find out.

Think It Over

Observing What happened to the cork in Step 4? How is the cork's movement similar to the wave's movement? How is it different? Draw a diagram of what you see. Use arrows to show the movement of the cork.

GUIDE FOR READING

◆ What causes waves?

◆ What are the three main types of waves?

Reading Tip Before you read, think of what comes to mind when you hear the word *wave*. As you read, write a definition of a wave.

Far out to sea, the wind disturbs the calm surface of the water. A ripple forms. As the wind continues to blow, the ripple grows into a powerful wave that can travel a great distance. Near the beach, surfers wait eagerly. They quickly paddle into deeper water to catch the monstrous wave. Surfers enjoy the power of nature as they ride the wave to the shore.

What are waves? How can they travel so far? Why are some waves more powerful than others? In this section, you will explore how waves begin and how they move.

Waves and Energy

Waves crashing on a beach show the tremendous energy waves can carry. A **wave** is a disturbance that transfers energy from place to place. In science, **energy** is defined as the ability to do work. To understand waves, think of a boat out on the ocean. If a wave disturbs the surface of the water, it will cause anything floating on the water to be disturbed, too. The energy carried by a wave can lift even a large ship as it passes.

The disturbance caused by a wave is temporary. After the wave has passed, the water is calm again.

◀ A surfer riding a wave

What Carries Waves? Many waves require something to travel through. Water waves travel along the surface of the water and sound waves travel through air. You can even make a wave travel along a rope. The material through which a wave travels is called a **medium.** Gases (such as air), liquids (such as water), and solids (such as ropes) all act as mediums. Waves that require a medium through which to travel are called **mechanical waves.**

Although waves travel through a medium, they do not carry the medium itself with them. Look at the duck in Figure 1. When a wave moves under the duck, the duck moves up and down. It does not move along the surface of the water. After the wave passes, the water and the duck return to where they started.

Breaking waves at a beach behave a little differently. When waves hit a beach, the water does actually move along with the wave. This happens because the water near the beach is shallow. As the wave hits the shore, the bottom of the wave drags along the ocean floor. The top of the wave continues to move forward. Eventually the wave topples over, turning white and frothy as it breaks.

Not all waves require a medium to carry them along. Light from the sun, for example, can travel through empty space. Light is an example of an electromagnetic wave. You will learn more about electromagnetic waves in Chapter 3.

What Causes Waves? You can create waves by dipping your finger in water. **Waves are created when a source of energy causes a medium to vibrate.** A **vibration** is a repeated back-and-forth or up-and-down motion. This motion is the source of the wave.

A moving object has energy. The moving object can transfer energy to a nearby medium, creating a wave. For example, as the propellers of a motorboat turn, they disturb the calm water surface. The boat's propeller transfers energy to the water. The propeller produces a wave that travels through the water. As the boat moves through the water, it also causes waves.

☑️ *Checkpoint* *What are mechanical waves?*

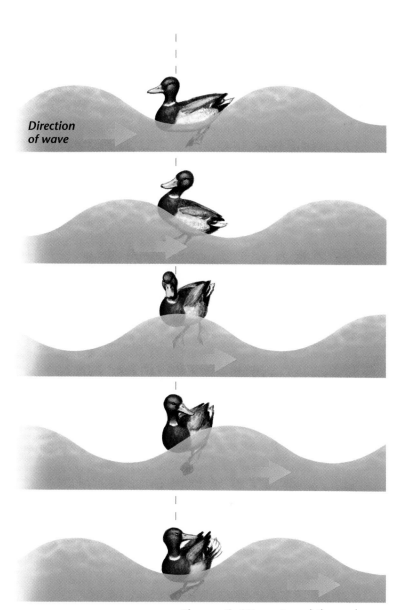

Direction of wave

Figure 1 Waves travel through water, but they do not carry the water with them. The duck moves up and down as a wave passes under it. The duck does not travel along with the wave.
Interpreting Diagrams *If you add a sixth sketch to the diagram, which stage should it most resemble?*

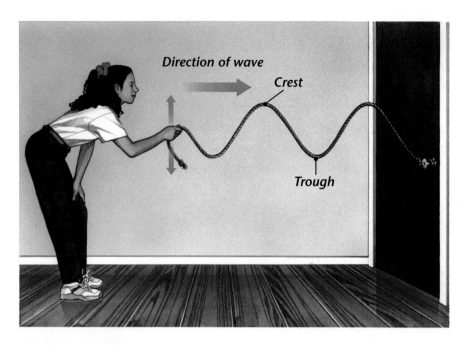

Figure 2 As she moves the free end of a rope up and down, the girl transfers energy to the rope. The energy travels along the rope, creating a transverse wave.

Direction of wave

Crest

Trough

Types of Waves

Different types of waves travel through mediums in different ways. **Waves are classified according to how they move. The three types of waves are transverse waves, longitudinal waves, and surface waves.**

Transverse Waves When you make a wave on a rope, the wave moves from one end of the rope to the other. The rope itself, however, moves up and down or from side to side. Waves that move the medium at right angles to the direction in which the waves are traveling are called **transverse waves.** Transverse means "across." As a transverse wave moves in one direction, the particles of the medium move across the direction of the wave. Figure 2 shows that some parts of the rope are very high while some are very low. The highest parts of the wave are called **crests,** and the lowest parts are called **troughs** (trawfs).

Figure 3 The coils in the spring toy move back and forth in the same direction as the motion of the wave. This is a longitudinal wave. *Comparing and Contrasting How does this wave compare with waves on a rope?*

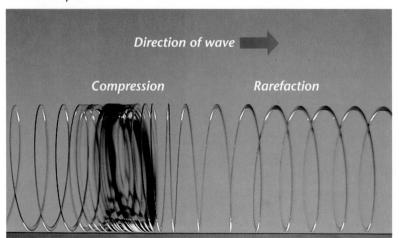

Direction of wave

Compression

Rarefaction

Longitudinal Waves Figure 3 shows a different kind of wave. If you stretch out a spring toy and push and pull one end, you can produce a longitudinal wave. **Longitudinal waves** (lawn juh TOO duh nul) move the particles of the medium parallel to the direction that the waves are traveling. The coils in the spring move back and forth in the same direction as the wave travels.

Notice in Figure 3 that in some parts of the spring the coils are close together. In

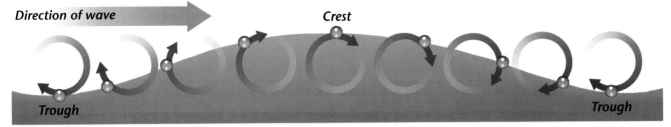

Direction of wave

Crest

Trough

Trough

Figure 4 In a surface wave, up-and-down motion combines with back-and-forth motion. The combination produces circular motion.

other parts, the coils are more spread out. The parts where the coils are close together are called **compressions** (kum PRESH uns). The parts where the coils are spread out, or rarefied, are called **rarefactions** (rair uh FAK shunz).

As compressions and rarefactions travel along the spring toy, each coil moves slightly forward and then back. The energy travels from one end of the spring to the other, creating a wave. After the wave passes, each part of the spring returns to the position where it started.

Combinations of Waves **Surface waves** are combinations of transverse and longitudinal waves. These waves occur at the surface between two mediums, such as water and air. When a wave passes through water, the water (and anything on it) moves up and down, like a transverse wave on a rope. The water also moves back and forth slightly in the direction that the wave is traveling, like the coils of the spring. But unlike the coils of a spring, water does not compress. The up-and-down and back-and-forth movements combine to make each particle of water move in a circle. Figure 4 shows the circular motion of surface waves.

Section 1 Review

1. Where do waves get their energy?
2. Name the three types of waves. Give an example of each type.
3. When a wave passes a ship at sea, how does the wave affect the ship?
4. **Thinking Critically** **Applying Concepts** The vibrations produced by a jackhammer are used to break up pavement. What type of waves do you think the jackhammer produces in the ground? Explain.

Check Your Progress

CHAPTER PROJECT 1

Find and list as many examples of periodic motion as you can. Look for cycles and patterns that repeat in only a few seconds and others that take hours or days to repeat. Try to find examples that continue day after day, such as the rising and setting of the sun. Don't limit your search to your home or school. Look at the world around you and at the solar system for ideas. Describe and sketch each example you find.

SECTION
② Properties of Waves

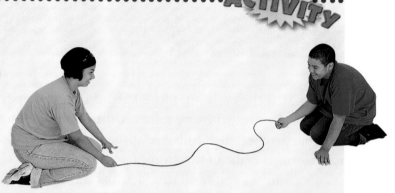

DISCOVER ·······················ACTIVITY···

How Can You Change a Wave?

1. Lay a rope about 3 meters long on a smooth floor. Securely hold one end. Have a partner hold the other end.

2. Flick the end of the rope left and right about once per second to make a series of waves travel down the rope. Observe the waves as they travel toward your partner.

3. Now flick the end of the rope more often— about two times per second. Again, observe the waves.

4. Switch roles with your partner and repeat Steps 2 and 3.

Think It Over

Predicting What happened to the waves when you flicked the rope more often? How will the wave change if you flick the rope less often than once per second? Try it.

GUIDE FOR READING

◆ **What are the basic properties of waves?**

◆ **How is a wave's speed related to its wavelength and frequency?**

Reading Tip As you read, make a list of the properties of waves. Write a sentence that describes each property.

Rhythmic gymnastics ▶

One of the most elegant and graceful Olympic sports is rhythmic gymnastics. A ribbon dancer flicks a stick attached to a ribbon, making waves travel down the ribbon. Some of the waves are long, while others are shorter. The rate at which the gymnast flicks her hands affects the length and shape of the waves in the ribbon.

There are many different kinds of waves. Waves can carry a little energy or a lot. They can be short or long. They can be rare or frequent. They can travel fast or slow. All waves, however, share certain properties. **The basic properties of waves are amplitude, wavelength, frequency, and speed.**

Wave Diagrams

To understand the properties of waves, it helps to represent a wave on a diagram. Transverse waves like those on a rope are easy to draw. You can draw a transverse wave as shown in Figure 5. Think of the horizontal line as the position of the rope before it is disturbed. This is its rest position. As the wave passes, the rope goes above or below the rest position. Remember that the crests and the troughs are the highest and lowest points on the wave.

To draw longitudinal waves, think of the compressions in the spring toy as being similar to the crests of a transverse wave. The rarefactions in the spring toy are like the troughs of a transverse wave. By treating compressions as crests and rarefactions as troughs, you can draw longitudinal waves in the same way as transverse waves.

✓ *Checkpoint* *Which part of a longitudinal wave is similar to the crest of a transverse wave?*

Amplitude

Some waves are very high, while others are barely noticeable. The distance the water rises depends on the amplitude of the wave that passes through it. **Amplitude** is the maximum distance the medium carrying the wave moves away from its rest position. The amplitude is a measure of how much a particle in the medium moves when disturbed by the wave. The amplitude of a water wave is the maximum distance a water particle moves above or below the surface level of calm water.

You know that waves are produced by something vibrating. The farther the medium moves as it vibrates, the larger the amplitude of the resulting waves. You can increase the amplitude of the waves on a rope by moving your hand up and down a greater distance. To do this, you have to use more energy. This greater amount of energy is then transferred to the rope. Thus, the amplitude of a wave is a direct measure of its energy.

Amplitude of Transverse Waves Compare the two transverse waves in Figure 6. You can see that wave A goes up and down a greater distance than wave B. The amplitude of a transverse wave is the maximum distance the medium moves up or down from its rest position. You can find the amplitude of a transverse wave by measuring the distance from the rest position to a crest or to a trough.

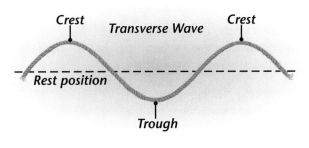
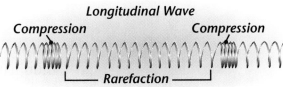

Figure 5 The crests and troughs of a transverse wave are the points at which the medium is farthest from the rest position. The compressions of a longitudinal wave correspond to the crests of a transverse wave.

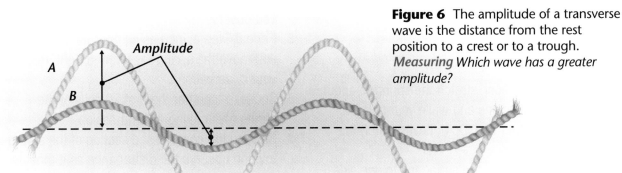

Figure 6 The amplitude of a transverse wave is the distance from the rest position to a crest or to a trough. *Measuring Which wave has a greater amplitude?*

Figure 7 If the compressions of a longitudinal wave are very crowded, the wave has a large amplitude.
Interpreting Diagrams Which longitudinal wave shown has the larger amplitude?

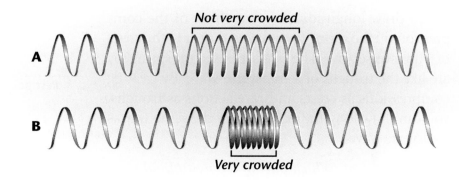

Amplitude of Longitudinal Waves The amplitude of a longitudinal wave is a measure of how compressed or rarefied the medium becomes. High-energy vibrations cause the compressions to be very crowded. This makes the rarefactions quite loose. Crowded compressions and uncrowded rarefactions are like high crests and low troughs. They mean that the longitudinal wave has a large amplitude.

Skills Lab

Observing

Wavy Motions

*N*ow it's your turn to make some waves on a spring toy. In this lab, you will observe some properties of waves.

Problem

How do waves travel in a spring toy?

Materials (per group)

spring toy   meter stick

Procedure

1. On a smooth floor, stretch the spring to about 3 meters. Hold one end while your partner holds the other end. Do not overstretch the spring toy.
2. Pull a few coils of the spring toy to one side near one end of the spring.
3. Release the coils and observe the motion of the spring. What happens when the disturbance reaches your partner? Draw what you observe.
4. Have your partner move one end of the spring toy to the left and then to the right on the floor. Be certain to hold both ends of the spring securely. Draw a diagram of the wave you observe.
5. Repeat Step 4, increasing the rate at which you move the spring toy left and right. Record your observations.
6. Squeeze together the first 20 coils of the spring toy, making a compression.
7. Release the compressed section of the spring toy and observe the disturbance as it moves down the spring. Record your observations. Draw and label what you see.

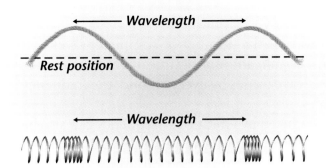

Wavelength

Rest position

Wavelength

Figure 8 The wavelength of a transverse wave is the distance from crest to crest. The wavelength of a longitudinal wave is the distance from compression to compression.

Wavelength

A wave travels a certain distance before it starts to repeat. The distance between two corresponding parts of a wave is its **wavelength.** You can find the wavelength of a transverse wave by measuring the distance from crest to crest or from trough to trough. You can find the wavelength of a longitudinal wave by measuring the distance from one compression to the next.

Analyze and Conclude

1. Compare the waves generated in Steps 1–5 with the waves generated in Steps 6–7.
2. Were the waves generated in Steps 1–5 transverse or longitudinal? Explain your answer.
3. In Step 3 of the procedure, compare the original wave to the wave that came back.
4. Were the waves generated in Steps 6 and 7 transverse or longitudinal? Explain your answer.
5. What happened to the wavelength and frequency when you increased the rate at which the spring toy moved left and right?
6. How did you change the amplitude of the waves you made?
7. **Think About It** Based on your observations, describe two ways that waves move through a spring toy. Use drawings and written explanations.

More to Explore

Obtain a wide variety of spring toys. Look for different sizes and materials, such as metal and plastic. Explore the differences among the waves you can produce on each spring. What accounts for these differences?

Frequency

The **frequency** of a wave is the number of complete waves that pass a given point in a certain amount of time. If you make waves on a rope so that one wave passes by every second, the frequency is 1 wave per second.

Since waves are produced by vibrations, frequency can also be described as the number of vibrations per second. To increase the frequency of the waves on a rope, you can move your hand up and down more often, perhaps two or three times per second. To decrease the frequency, you move your hand less often, perhaps once every two or three seconds.

Frequency is measured in units called **hertz (Hz)**. A wave or vibration that occurs every second has a frequency of 1 Hz. If two waves pass you every second, then the frequency of the wave is 2 per second, or 2 hertz. The hertz was named after the German scientist Heinrich Hertz, who first produced radio waves.

☑ *Checkpoint* *How can you increase the frequency of waves on a rope?*

Speed

Imagine watching a distant thunderstorm on a hot summer day. First you see the flash of lightning. A few seconds later you hear the roll of thunder. Even though the lightning and thunder occurred at the same instant, they reach you seconds apart. This happens because sound and light travel at very different speeds. Light travels much faster than sound. Different waves travel at different speeds. The speed of a wave is how far the wave travels in one unit of time, or distance divided by time.

The speed, wavelength, and frequency of a wave are related to each other by a mathematical formula.

$$Speed = Wavelength \times Frequency$$

If you know any two of the quantities in the speed formula—speed, wavelength, and frequency—you can calculate the third quantity. For example, if you know the speed and the wavelength of a wave, you can calculate the frequency. If you know the speed and the frequency, you can calculate the wavelength.

$$Frequency = \frac{Speed}{Wavelength} \qquad Wavelength = \frac{Speed}{Frequency}$$

Waves in different mediums travel at different speeds. In a given medium and under the same conditions, the speed of a wave is constant. For example, all sound waves traveling through the air at the same pressure and at the same temperature travel

Math TOOLBOX

Calculating With Units

When calculating with quantities that include units, treat the units as you do the numbers.

For example, if an object travels 6 m in 2 s, here is how you find its speed:

$$Speed = \frac{Distance}{Time}$$

$$= \frac{6\ m}{2\ s}$$

$$= 3\ m/s$$

A wave on a lake has a wavelength of 0.5 m and a frequency of 2 Hz (2 Hz = 2 per second, or 2/s). To find the speed of the wave, use this formula:

$$Speed = Wavelength \times Frequency$$

Substitute and simplify:

$$Speed = 0.5\ m \times 2\ Hz$$

$$= 0.5\ m \times 2\ /s$$

$$= 1\ m/s$$

The speed of the wave is 1 m/s. Note that the answer is in meters per second, which is a correct unit for speed.

at the same speed. If the temperature or pressure changes, the sound waves will travel at a different speed.

If the same type of wave travels at the same speed in the same medium, what do you think will happen if the frequency changes? When you multiply the wavelength and frequency after the change, you should get the same speed as before the change. Therefore, if you increase the frequency of a wave, the wavelength must decrease.

Sample Problem

The speed of a wave on a rope is 50 cm/s and its wavelength is 10 cm. What is the frequency?

Analyze.   You know speed and wavelength. You want to find frequency.

Write the formula. $\text{Frequency} = \dfrac{Speed}{Wavelength}$

Substitute and solve. $\text{Frequency} = \dfrac{50 \ \cancel{cm}/s}{10 \ \cancel{cm}}$

$\text{Frequency} = \dfrac{5\cancel{0} \ /s}{1\cancel{0}}$

$\text{Frequency} = 5 \ /s$ (5 per second) or 5 Hz.

Think about it.   If you move your hand as often as 5 times a second, then fairly short waves, only 10 cm long, will move down the rope.

Practice Problems

1. A wave has a wavelength of 5 mm and a frequency of 2 Hz. At what speed does the wave travel?

2. The speed of a wave on a guitar string is 100 m/s and the frequency is 1,000 Hz. What is the wavelength of the wave?

Section 2 Review

1. List the four basic properties of waves. Describe each property.
2. How are the speed, wavelength, and frequency of a wave related?
3. Can two waves have the same wavelength but different amplitudes? Explain.
4. **Thinking Critically Inferring** When you increase the tension on a piece of wire, the speed of waves on it increases, but the wavelength stays constant. What happens to the frequency of the waves as the tension on the wire is increased?

Check Your Progress

CHAPTER PROJECT
1

Observe the amplitude, wavelength, frequency, and speed of one of the periodic motions on your list. How many complete repetitions of each periodic motion occur in a given amount of time? How long it does it take for a periodic event to finish and start again? Compare the highest and lowest position or the nearest and farthest position of the object showing periodic motion. Record your observations in your notebook.

SECTION
3 Interactions of Waves

DISCOVER ‧‧‧‧‧‧‧‧‧‧‧‧‧‧‧‧‧‧‧‧‧‧‧‧‧‧‧‧‧‧‧‧‧‧‧‧‧‧ ACTIVITY

How Does a Ball Bounce?

1. Choose a spot at the base of a wall. From a distance of 1 m, roll a wet ball along the floor straight at the spot you chose. Watch the angle at which the ball bounces back by looking at the path of moisture on the floor.

2. Wet the ball again. From a different position, roll the ball at the same spot, but at an angle to the wall. Again, observe the angle at which the ball bounces back.

Think It Over

Developing Hypotheses How do you think the angle at which the ball hits the wall is related to the angle at which the ball bounces back? To test your hypothesis, roll the ball from several different positions toward the same spot on the wall.

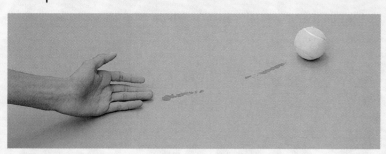

GUIDE FOR READING

◆ How do waves bend?

◆ How do waves interact with each other?

Reading Tip Before you read, preview *Exploring Interactions of Waves* on pages 28–29. Make a list of any unfamiliar words you find there. As you read, write a definition for each word on your list.

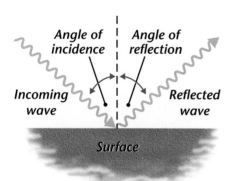

Figure 9 The angle of reflection is equal to the angle of incidence.

It is a hot, sunny day. You are the first person to enter the calm water of the swimming pool. To test the temperature of the water, you dip one foot in first. Your foot causes a series of ripples to travel across the water to the far wall of the pool. As each ripple hits the wall, it bounces off the wall and travels back toward you.

Reflection

When water waves hit the side of a swimming pool, they bounce back. **When an object or wave hits a surface through which it cannot pass, it bounces back.** This is called **reflection.**

To show reflection of a wave, draw a line in the direction of the motion of the wave. Now imagine a line perpendicular to the wall or surface. The **angle of incidence** is the angle between the incoming wave and the imaginary perpendicular line. The **angle of reflection** is the angle between the reflected wave and the imaginary line. The law of reflection states that the angle of reflection equals the angle of incidence. All waves obey the law of reflection.

There are many examples of reflection in your everyday life. A ball that hits a wall bounces back, or is reflected. When you look in a mirror, you use reflected light to see yourself. An echo is an example of reflected sound.

Refraction

Have you ever pushed a shopping cart that had a stiff wheel? If so, you know how difficult it is to control the direction of the cart. This is because the stiff wheel can't turn as fast as the other wheels. As you push the cart, it tends to veer to the side of the sticky wheel and so changes direction. Waves sometimes change direction when they enter a new medium. If a wave enters the new medium at an angle, one side changes speed before the other side. **When a wave moves from one medium into another medium at an angle, it changes speed as it enters the second medium, which causes it to bend.** The bending of waves due to a change in speed is called **refraction.**

Though all waves change speed when they enter a new medium, they don't always bend. Bending occurs when one side of the wave enters the new medium before the other side of the wave. The side of the wave that enters the new medium first changes speed first. The other side is still traveling at its original speed. The bending occurs because the two sides of the wave are traveling at different speeds.

✓ *Checkpoint* What is refraction?

Diffraction

Sometimes waves can bend around an obstacle in their path. For example, waves can pass through a narrow entrance to a harbor and then spread out inside the harbor. Figure 10 shows water waves diffracting as they enter a harbor.

When a wave passes a barrier or moves through a hole in a barrier, it bends and spreads out. The bending of waves

Figure 10 Waves from the ocean enter the harbor and spread out. This is an example of diffraction. *Predicting How do you think the waves in the harbor would change if the opening were wider?*

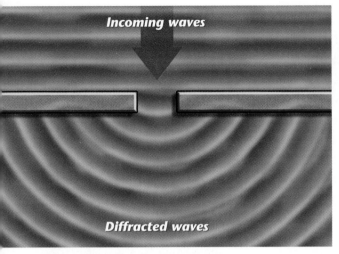

Incoming waves

Diffracted waves

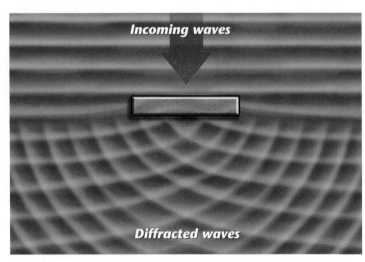

Incoming waves

Diffracted waves

Figure 11 The diagram shows how waves diffract. A wave can go through a hole in a barrier and spread out (left). Or it can bend around a barrier (right).

around the edge of a barrier is known as **diffraction.** Figure 11 shows a water wave passing through a hole in a barrier and another bending around a barrier. In each case, you see the wave diffracting on the other side of the barrier.

☑ *Checkpoint* *What is diffraction?*

Interference

Suppose that you and a friend are each holding one end of a rope. If you both flick the ends at the same time, you send two waves toward each other. What will happen when those two waves meet?

When two or more waves meet, they have an effect on each other. This interaction is called **interference.** There are two types of interference: constructive and destructive.

Constructive Interference **Constructive interference** occurs whenever two waves combine to make a wave with a larger amplitude. You can think of constructive interference as waves "helping each other" to give a stronger result, or adding energy.

Figure 12 shows two identical waves (same amplitude, same wavelength) traveling in the same direction at the same time. If the two waves travel along the same path at the same time, they will behave as one. What will the combined wave look like? The crests of the first wave will occur at the same place as the crests of the second wave. The energy from the two waves will combine. Thus the amplitude of the new wave will be twice the amplitude of either of the original waves.

If the waves have the same wavelength but different amplitudes, the crests will still occur at the same place and add together. The resulting amplitude will be the sum of the two original amplitudes. Similarly, the troughs will occur together, making a deeper trough than either wave alone.

Figure 12 The diagrams show how identical waves can combine.

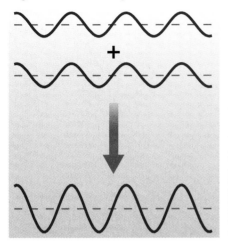

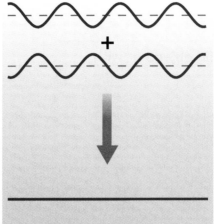

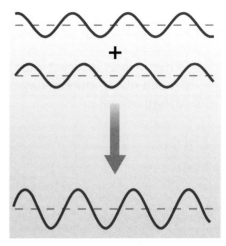

A. When the crests align, the waves add together and produce a wave with twice the original amplitude.

B. When the crests of one wave align with the troughs of another, they cancel each other out.

C. If one wave travels a little behind the other, they combine both constructively and destructively at different places.

Destructive Interference When the amplitudes of two waves combine with each other producing a smaller amplitude, the result is called **destructive interference.** What happens if the crests don't meet at the same place? In this case, one wave comes after the other. Figure 12B shows what happens when the crests of the first wave occur at the same place as the troughs of the second wave. The amplitude of the first wave cancels out the amplitude of the second wave. This type of interference produces a wave with an amplitude of zero. The original waves seem to be destroyed. If the two waves have different amplitudes, they will not cancel each other out but will combine to produce a wave with a smaller amplitude.

Two identical waves can travel along the same path, one a little behind the other. When this happens, the waves combine constructively in some places and destructively in others.

Standing Waves

If you tie a rope to a doorknob and continuously shake the free end, waves will travel down the rope, reflect at the end, and come back. The reflected waves will collide with the incoming waves. When the waves meet, interference occurs. After they pass each other, they carry on as if the interference had never occurred.

If the incoming wave and the reflected wave combine at the right places, the combined wave appears to be standing still. A **standing wave** is a wave that appears to stand in one place, even though it is really two waves interfering as they pass through each other. If you make a standing wave on a rope, the rope looks as though it is standing still. But in fact, waves are traveling along the rope in both directions.

Standing Waves

Here's how you can make a standing wave.

1. Tie a piece of elastic cord about 3 m long to a fixed, solid object. Hold the cord securely and pull it tight.

2. Slowly move the end of the cord up and down until you produce a standing wave.

3. Now move the cord up and down twice as fast to double the frequency. What happens?

Predicting What do you think will happen if you triple the original frequency? Try it. Be careful to keep a good grip on the cord.

EXPLORING Interactions of Waves

When waves interact with solid objects or with each other, they behave in a variety of ways.

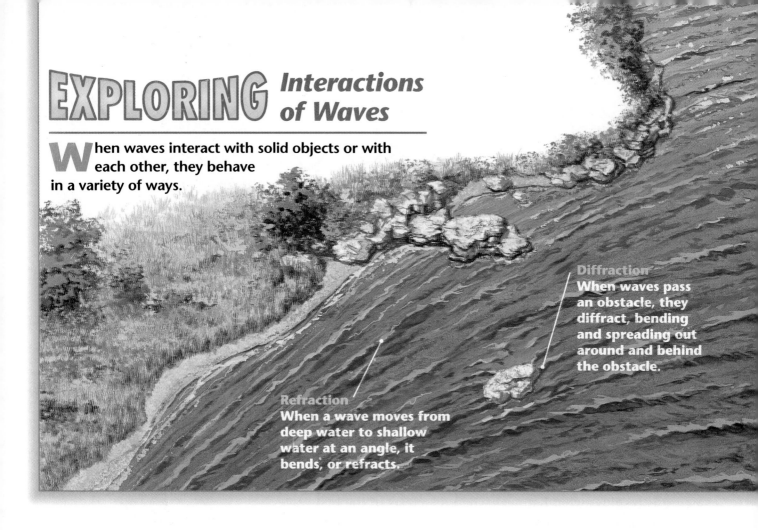

Diffraction
When waves pass an obstacle, they diffract, bending and spreading out around and behind the obstacle.

Refraction
When a wave moves from deep water to shallow water at an angle, it bends, or refracts.

Nodes and Antinodes At certain points, destructive interference causes the two waves to combine to produce an amplitude of zero, as in Figure 13. These points are called **nodes.** The nodes always occur at the same place on the rope. The diagram also shows how the amplitudes of the two waves combine to produce amplitudes greater than zero. The crests and troughs of the standing wave are called **antinodes.** These are the points of maximum energy.

Resonance Have you ever pushed a child on a swing? At first, it is difficult to push the swing. But once you get it going, you need only push gently to keep it going. When an object is vibrating at a certain frequency, it takes very little energy to maintain or increase the amplitude of the wave.

Most objects have a natural frequency of vibration. Their particles vibrate naturally at a certain frequency. **Resonance** occurs when vibrations traveling through an object match the object's natural frequency. If vibrations of the same frequency are added, the amplitude of the object's vibrations increases.

Figure 13 A standing wave is set up when the reflected wave interacts with the incoming wave. The nodes are the points of zero amplitude. The antinodes are the points of maximum amplitude.

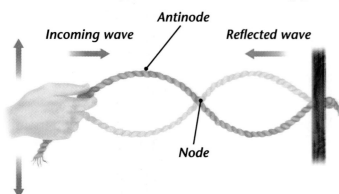

Incoming wave

Antinode

Reflected wave

Node

Constructive Interference When two waves combine to make a wave with a larger amplitude, the result is constructive interference.

Destructive Interference When two waves combine to make a wave with a smaller amplitude, the result is destructive interference.

Reflection When a wave hits a barrier, it reflects at the same angle that it hit the barrier.

An object that is vibrating at its natural frequency absorbs energy from objects that vibrate at the same frequency. Resonance occurs in music and adds a distinct quality to the sound.

If an object is not very flexible, resonance can cause it to shatter. For this reason, marching troops are told to break step as they cross a bridge. If they all march across the bridge in perfect step, it is possible that the pounding could match the natural frequency of the bridge. The increased vibration could cause the bridge to collapse.

Section 3 Review

1. What is the law of reflection?
2. What causes refraction?
3. Describe the difference between constructive and destructive interference.
4. What causes a standing wave?
5. **Thinking Critically** **Predicting** Two water waves have the same wavelength. The crests of one occur at the same place as the crests of the second. If one wave has twice the amplitude of the other, will the waves interfere constructively or destructively? Explain.

Science at Home

With your parent's permission, fill the kitchen sink with water to a depth of about 10 cm. Dip your finger in the water repeatedly to make waves. Demonstrate reflection and interference to your family members. Try to think of ways to demonstrate refraction and diffraction as well.

Making Waves

In this lab, you will use a model to investigate wave behavior.

Problem

How do water waves interact with each other and with solid objects in their paths?

Materials

water	plastic dropper
metric ruler	paper towel
modeling clay	

cork or other small floating object

ripple tank (aluminum foil lasagna pan with mirror at the bottom)

Procedure

Part 1 Water Drops

1. Fill the pan with water to a depth of 1.5 cm. Let the water come to rest.
2. Lift one end of the ripple tank about 4 cm and quickly set it back down. Watch the motion of the water until it settles down. Record your observations in a table like the one below.
3. Fill a plastic dropper with water. From a height of about 10 cm, release a drop of water into the center of the ripple tank and observe the waves. Then release drops of water from the same height at various locations away from the center of the tank.

4. Continue dropping water into the tank.
   a. What happens when waves hit the side of the tank? What happens when two waves hit each other?
   b. How can you change the amplitude? The wavelength? The frequency?
   c. What variables can you change to observe different wave behavior?
5. Predict what would happen to the amplitude of the waves if you change the height from which you release the drops.
6. Release another drop from a height of 20 cm and one from a height of 5 cm. Record your observations.
7. Predict how placing a paper towel at one end of the tank will affect wave reflections.
8. Drape a paper towel across one end of the ripple tank so that it hangs in the water. Repeat Steps 3–6 and record your observations.

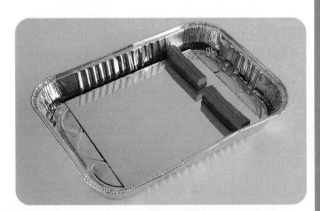

DATA TABLE

Height of Dropper (cm)	Horizontal Distance From Center of Tank (cm)	Observations	
		No Barrier	Barrier

Part 2 Barriers

9. Remove the paper towel and place a stick of modeling clay in the water near the center of the tank. Make some more waves with the dropper. Observe what happens when waves traveling from the end of the tank strike the clay.

10. Place the clay in different positions so that the waves strike it at different angles. Record all observations in your notebook.

11. Place two sticks of clay end-to-end across the ripple tank to make a barrier with a 2-cm gap in the middle. Observe and record what happens when waves hit the barrier and the opening in the barrier. Change the position of the barrier in the pan. Observe any differences.

12. Now make a barrier having two 2-cm gaps that are 5 cm apart. Observe and record what happens when waves hit the barrier and the opening in the barrier.

13. Add a small floating object, such as a cork, to the water and repeat Steps 9–12. Observe and record what happens to the cork at each step.

14. Make sure you wipe up all spills when you are done.

Analyze and Conclude

1. How is the wave made by lifting one side of the tank different from the waves made with the plastic dropper?

2. How does the height from which the drops fall affect the waves that are produced?

3. How are waves affected by the paper towel hanging in the water?

4. What happens when waves strike a barrier head on? When they strike it at an angle?

5. What happens when waves strike a barrier with a gap in it? With two gaps in it?

6. **Think About It** How does the behavior of waves in your model compare to the behavior of waves in a harbor?

Design an Experiment

Predict what would happen if you could send a steady train of uniform waves the length of the tank for an extended time. Use a plastic bottle with a pinhole in the bottom to make a model that will help to test your prediction. Get permission from your teacher to try out your dropper device.

SECTION 4 Seismic Waves

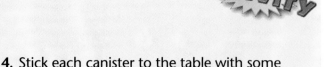

DISCOVER

Can You Find the Sand?

1. Fill a plastic film canister with sand and replace the lid tightly.

2. Place the canister on a table with four other identical but empty canisters. Mix them around so that a classmate does not know which can is which.

3. With your fist, pound on the table a few times. Have your classmate try to figure out which canister contains the sand.

4. Stick each canister to the table with some modeling clay. Pound on the table again. Now can your classmate figure out which canister contains the sand?

Think It Over
Inferring Pounding on a table makes waves. Why might the canister containing the sand respond differently from the empty canisters?

GUIDE FOR READING

◆ What happens when rock beneath Earth's surface moves?

◆ What are the different types of seismic waves?

◆ How does a seismograph work?

Reading Tip As you read, make a table comparing primary, secondary, and surface waves.

Some of the most dramatic waves originate deep inside Earth. On August 27, 1883, the eruption of Krakatau volcano in Indonesia caused a series of earthquakes. Vibrations from the earthquakes formed waves that traveled from the island through the surrounding water. On the open ocean, the waves were only about 1 meter high. As they entered shallower water, near land, the waves traveled more slowly. This caused the waves to catch up with each other and combine. The first wave grew into a wall of water over 35 meters high. People on ships far out at sea could not even tell when the waves went by. But on the islands of Java and Sumatra thousands of people were killed as the enormous waves crashed onto the land.

Figure 14 This illustration shows a giant wave reaching the coast of Java. The wave was caused by earthquakes related to the eruption of Krakatau volcano 40 kilometers away.

Types of Seismic Waves

An earthquake occurs when rock beneath Earth's surface moves. The movement of Earth's plates creates stress in the rock. **When the stress in the rock builds up enough, the rock breaks or changes shape, releasing energy in the form of waves or vibrations.** The waves produced by earthquakes are known as **seismic waves.** (The word *seismic* comes from the Greek word *seismos*, meaning "earthquake.")

Seismic waves ripple out in all directions from the point where the earthquake occurred. As the waves move, they carry the energy through Earth. The waves can travel from one side of Earth to the other. **Seismic waves include primary waves, secondary waves, and surface waves.**

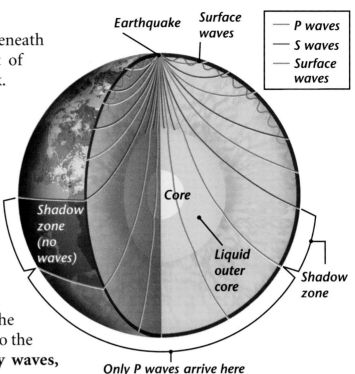

Only P waves arrive here

Figure 15 P waves travel through all parts of Earth. S waves do not travel through Earth's core. Surface waves travel only along Earth's surface. The shadow zone is where there are no seismic waves.
Applying Concepts Why don't S waves travel through Earth's core?

Primary Waves Some seismic waves are longitudinal waves. Longitudinal seismic waves are known as **primary waves,** or P waves. They are called primary waves because they move faster than other seismic waves and so arrive at distant points before other seismic waves. Primary waves are made up of compressions and rarefactions of rock inside Earth.

Secondary Waves Other seismic waves are transverse waves with crests and troughs. Transverse seismic waves are known as **secondary waves,** or S waves. Secondary waves cannot travel through liquids. Since part of Earth's core is liquid, S waves do not travel directly through Earth and cannot be detected on the side of Earth opposite an earthquake. Because of this, scientists on the side of Earth opposite the earthquake detect mainly P waves.

Surface Waves When P waves and S waves reach Earth's surface, some of them are transformed into surface waves similar to waves on the surface of water. Recall that surface waves are a combination of longitudinal and transverse waves. Even though surface waves travel more slowly than either P or S waves, they produce the most severe ground movements.

Earthquakes that occur underwater can cause huge surface waves on the ocean called **tsunamis** (tsoo NAH meez). Tsunamis can cause great damage when they reach land.

✓ *Checkpoint* *How are P waves different from S waves?*

Detecting Seismic Waves

If you did the Discover activity, you saw how waves can affect different masses by different amounts. To detect and measure earthquake waves, scientists use instruments called **seismographs** (SYZ muh grafs). **A seismograph records the ground movements caused by seismic waves as they move through Earth.**

The frame of the seismograph is attached to the ground, so the frame shakes when seismic waves arrive at the seismograph's location. Seismographs used to have pens attached to the frame that made wiggly lines on a roll of paper as the ground shook. Now scientists use electronic seismographs that use computers to record data about Earth's motion.

Since P waves travel through Earth faster than S waves, P waves arrive at seismographs before S waves. By measuring the time between the arrival of the P waves and the S waves, scientists can tell how far away the earthquake was. By comparing readings from at least three seismographs at different places on Earth, scientists can tell where the earthquake occurred.

INTEGRATING TECHNOLOGY Oil, water, minerals, and other valuable substances are hidden under Earth's surface. To find out what is under the ground, geologists may set off explosives to produce a small earthquake. The seismic waves from the explosion reflect from structures deep underground to seismographs located around the site of the explosion. The readings help geologists to locate mineral resources underground.

Figure 16 A scientist studies the printout from a seismograph.

Section 4 Review

1. What causes seismic waves?
2. Describe the different types of seismic waves.
3. How do seismographs help scientists determine where an earthquake occurred?
4. **Thinking Critically** **Inferring** S waves can travel from one side of the moon, through the core, to the other side. What does this tell you about the center of the moon? Explain.

Science at Home

Find out how disturbances travel through different solids. Have a family member or friend tap one end of the table with a spoon. Now put your ear down on the other side of the table and listen to the tapping again. What difference do you notice? Repeat the tapping on various surfaces around your home. What observations have you made?

SECTION 1 What Are Waves?

Key Ideas

◆ A wave is a disturbance that transfers energy from place to place.
◆ Transverse waves have crests and troughs. Longitudinal waves have compressions and rarefactions.
◆ Waves are created when a source of energy causes a medium to vibrate.
◆ Waves are classified according to how they move. The three types of waves are transverse waves, longitudinal waves, and surface waves.

Key Terms

wave   crest
energy   trough
medium   longitudinal wave
mechanical wave   compression
vibration   rarefaction
transverse wave   surface wave

SECTION 2 Properties of Waves

Key Ideas

◆ The basic properties of waves are amplitude, wavelength, frequency, and speed.
◆ The amplitude of a wave is the maximum distance that the particles of the medium move away from the rest position.
◆ The speed, frequency, and wavelength of a wave are related to each other by a mathematical formula.
Speed = Wavelength × Frequency

Key Terms

amplitude   frequency
wavelength   hertz (Hz)

SECTION 3 Interactions of Waves

Key Ideas

◆ When an object or wave hits a surface through which it cannot pass, it bounces back. The law of reflection states that the angle of reflection of a wave is equal to the angle of incidence.
◆ When a wave moves from one medium into another medium at an angle, it changes speed in the second medium and bends.
◆ When a wave passes a barrier or moves through a hole in a barrier, it bends and spreads out.
◆ When two or more waves meet, they can combine either constructively or destructively.

Key Terms

reflection   constructive interference
angle of incidence   destructive interference
angle of reflection   standing wave
refraction   node
diffraction   antinode
interference   resonance

SECTION 4 Seismic Waves

INTEGRATING EARTH SCIENCE

Key Ideas

◆ When stress in the rock beneath Earth's surface builds up enough, the rock breaks or changes shape, releasing energy in the form of seismic waves.
◆ Seismic waves include primary waves, secondary waves, and surface waves.
◆ A seismograph records the ground movements caused by seismic waves as they move through Earth.

Key Terms

seismic wave   tsunami
primary wave   seismograph
secondary wave

USING THE INTERNET ACTIVITY

www.science-explorer.phschool.com

Reviewing Content

 For more review of key concepts, see the Interactive Student Tutorial CD-ROM.

Multiple Choice

Choose the letter of the best answer.

1. A wave carries
   a. energy.   b. matter.
   c. water.   d. air.
2. The distance between one crest and the next crest is the wave's
   a. amplitude.
   b. wavelength.
   c. frequency.
   d. speed.
3. In a given medium, if the frequency of a wave increases, its
   a. wavelength increases.
   b. speed increases.
   c. amplitude decreases.
   d. wavelength decreases.
4. The bending of a wave due to a change in its speed is
   a. interference.
   b. diffraction.
   c. reflection.
   d. refraction.
5. Seismic waves that do *not* travel through liquids are
   a. P waves.
   b. S waves.
   c. surface waves.
   d. tsunamis.

True or False

If the statement is true, write true. If it is false, change the underlined word or words to make the statement true.

6. <u>Transverse</u> waves have compressions and rarefactions.
7. When the particles of a medium move a great distance as the wave passes, the wave has a large <u>amplitude</u>.
8. When a wave changes speed as it enters a new medium, it undergoes <u>diffraction</u>.
9. Nodes and antinodes occur in <u>longitudinal</u> waves.
10. <u>Secondary</u> waves arrive at distant points before other seismic waves.

Checking Concepts

11. Explain the difference between transverse and longitudinal waves. Use diagrams to illustrate your explanation.
12. How can you find the amplitude of a longitudinal wave?
13. How are a wave's speed, wavelength, and frequency related?
14. Describe the difference between constructive and destructive interference.
15. Explain how seismographs work.
16. **Writing to Learn** Suppose you are a sportswriter with a background in science. While at a baseball game, you notice that at various times, entire sections of people stand up and sit down again. This "wave" travels around the stadium. Write a short newspaper article that describes what the crowd is doing. Be sure to use terms such as amplitude, frequency, wavelength, and speed in your description. Give your article a title.

Thinking Visually

17. **Concept Map** Copy the concept map about waves onto a separate sheet of paper. Then complete it and add a title. (For more on concept maps, see the Skills Handbook.)

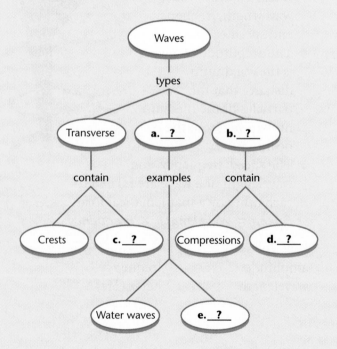

Applying Skills

The wave in the illustration is a giant ocean wave produced by an underwater earthquake. Use the illustration to answer Questions 18–21.

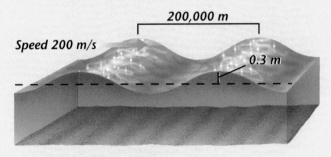

200,000 m

Speed 200 m/s

0.3 m

18. **Classifying** What kind of wave is this?
19. **Interpreting Diagrams** What is the amplitude of the wave shown? What is its speed? Find the frequency of the wave. Show your work.
20. **Predicting** What could happen if this wave hits a coastal city? What property of a wave determines how much damage it could do?
21. **Calculating** How long would it take this wave to travel 5,000 km?

Thinking Critically

22. **Comparing and Contrasting** One wave has half the amplitude of a second wave. The two waves interfere constructively. Draw a diagram and describe the resulting wave. Describe the resulting wave if two waves of equal amplitude interfere destructively.
23. **Calculating** A wave travels at 10 m/s and has a wavelength of 2 m. What is the frequency of the wave? If the speed of the wave doubles but the wavelength remains the same, what is the new frequency? Show your work.
24. **Making Models** Describe a way to model refraction of a wave as it enters a new medium.
25. **Applying Concepts** Suppose a wave moves from one side of a lake to the other. Does the water move across the lake? Explain.

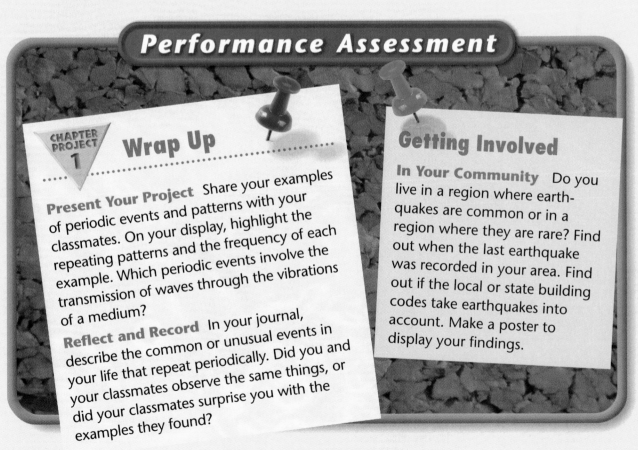

Performance Assessment

Wrap Up
CHAPTER PROJECT 1

Present Your Project Share your examples of periodic events and patterns with your classmates. On your display, highlight the repeating patterns and the frequency of each example. Which periodic events involve the transmission of waves through the vibrations of a medium?

Reflect and Record In your journal, describe the common or unusual events in your life that repeat periodically. Did you and your classmates observe the same things, or did your classmates surprise you with the examples they found?

Getting Involved

In Your Community Do you live in a region where earthquakes are common or in a region where they are rare? Find out when the last earthquake was recorded in your area. Find out if the local or state building codes take earthquakes into account. Make a poster to display your findings.

CHAPTER
2 Sound

 WHAT'S AHEAD

2 Music to Your Ears

Music, one of the oldest arts, forms an important part of many occasions. Early Chinese, Egyptian, and Babylonian people made stringed instruments from animal hair, whistles from bones, and trumpets from animal horns. Today, musical instruments are made of wood, brass, silver, and nylon.

In this chapter you will investigate the properties of sound. You will learn how sound is produced by different objects, including musical instruments. As you work through the chapter, you will gather enough knowledge to help you to complete the project.

Your Goal To design, build, and play a simple musical instrument.

To complete this project you must
- ◆ design a simple musical instrument
- ◆ construct and modify your instrument
- ◆ play a simple tune on your instrument

Get Started Begin now by discussing different kinds of instruments with your classmates. What kind of music do you enjoy? What instruments are common in your favorite type of music? Do you or any of your classmates already play an instrument? Which type of instrument would you like to build?

Check Your Progress You'll be working on this project as you study this chapter. To keep your project on track, look for Check Your Progress boxes at the following points.

Section 2 Review, page 51: Make a list of materials you could use to build your instrument.

Section 3 Review, page 59: Design and construct your instrument.
Section 5 Review, page 70: Test your instrument. Modify and test it again.

Wrap Up At the end of the chapter (page 73), you will demonstrate how you can vary the loudness and pitch of the sound of your instrument and play a simple tune.

These musical instruments play a part in African ceremonial life.

 Integrating Life Science

SECTION 4 How You Hear Sound

Discover Where Is the Sound Coming From?
Try This Listen to Sounds

SECTION 5 Applications of Sound

Discover How Can You Use Time to Measure Distance?
Sharpen Your Skills Observing

SECTION 1 The Nature of Sound

DISCOVER ··· ACTIVITY····

What Is Sound?

1. Fill a bowl with water.

2. Tap a tuning fork against the sole of your shoe. Place the tip of one of the prongs in the water. What do you see?

3. Tap the tuning fork again. Predict what will happen when you hold it near your ear. What do you hear?

Think It Over

Observing How do you think your observations are related to the sound you hear? What might change if you use a tuning fork of a different size? What would change in the sound you hear?

GUIDE FOR READING

◆ What is sound?

◆ What factors affect the speed of sound?

Reading Tip Before you read, preview the headings in the section. Record the headings in outline form, leaving room to add notes.

Here is an old riddle: If a tree falls in a forest and no one is there to hear it, does the tree make a sound? To answer the question, you must decide how to define the word "sound." If sound is something that a person must hear with his or her ears, then you might say that the tree makes no sound.

When a tree crashes down, the energy with which it strikes the forest floor is transmitted through the ground and the surrounding air. This energy causes the ground and the air to vibrate. If sound is a disturbance that travels through the ground or the air, then sound is created even if no one is around. So the tree does make a sound.

Sound and Longitudinal Waves

Just like the waves you studied in Chapter 1, sound begins with a vibration. When a tree crashes to the ground, the surrounding air particles are disturbed. This disturbance causes other vibrations in nearby particles.

How Sound Travels Like all waves, sound waves carry energy through a medium without the particles of the medium traveling along. A common medium for sound is air. Each molecule in the air moves back and forth as the disturbance goes by. **Sound is a disturbance that travels through a medium as a longitudinal wave.** When the disturbance reaches the air near your ears, you hear the sound.

How Sounds Are Made A drum also makes sounds by creating vibrations. When you beat a drum, the surface of the drum begins to vibrate so quickly that you cannot see it move. Air is

40 ◆ **O**

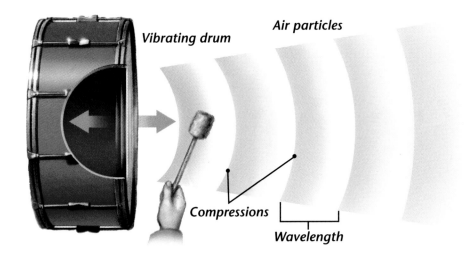

Vibrating drum

Air particles

Compressions

Wavelength

Figure 1 As the drum vibrates back and forth, it creates compressions and rarefactions in the air. *Classifying What type of wave does a drum make?*

mostly made up of tiny particles, or molecules, of gases. Figure 1 shows how the vibration of a drum creates a disturbance in the molecules in the air near it. When the drumhead moves to the right, it pushes the molecules together, creating a compression. When the drumhead moves to the left, the molecules move farther apart, creating a rarefaction.

When you pluck a guitar string, it vibrates back and forth, creating compressions and rarefactions. These compressions and rarefactions travel through the air as longitudinal waves similar to the longitudinal waves that you saw travel along a spring.

INTEGRATING LIFE SCIENCE Your vocal cords act like vibrating guitar strings. Whenever you speak or sing, you force air from your lungs up through your voice box, or **larynx.** Your larynx consists of two folds of tissue called vocal cords, shown in Figure 2. The forced air rushes by your vocal cords, making them vibrate. As your vocal cords move toward each other, the air between them is compressed. As they move apart, the air spreads out, or is rarefied. Like vibrating guitar strings, your vocal cords produce compressions and rarefactions in the air. The air carries these longitudinal waves to other people's ears as well as to your own.

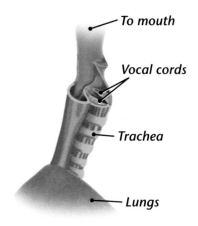

To mouth

Vocal cords

Trachea

Lungs

Figure 2 When a person speaks or sings, the vocal cords vibrate. The vibrations produce longitudinal sound waves in the air.

Sound in Solids and Liquids
Sound can also travel through solids and liquids. When you knock on a door, the particles of the door vibrate. The vibration creates sound waves that travel through the door. When the sound waves reach the other side of the door, they make sound waves in the air on the far side. In old western movies, you may see someone put an ear to a railway track to tell if

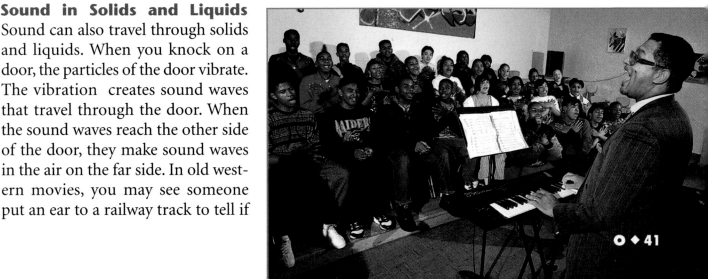

Figure 3 When sound waves enter a room through an open door, they spread out. This is called diffraction.

Figure 4 The speed of sound depends upon the medium through which it is traveling. *Making Generalizations In general, does sound travel faster in solids, liquids, or gases?*

Speed of Sound	
Medium	**Speed (m/s)**
Gases	
Air (0°C)	331
Air (20°C)	340
Liquids	
Fresh water	1,490
Salt water	1,531
Solids (25°C)	
Lead	1,210
Plastic	1,800
Silver	2,680
Copper	3,100
Gold	3,240
Brick	3,650
Hard wood	4,000
Glass	4,540
Iron	5,000
Steel	5,200

a train is on the way. The sound of the train travels easily through the steel tracks. If you put your ear to the ground, you might hear distant traffic. Sound waves from the traffic are traveling through the ground as well as through the air.

Sound can travel only if there is a medium to transmit the compressions and rarefactions. In outer space, there are no molecules to compress or rarefy. The energy of the original vibrations has nothing through which to travel. So sound does not travel through outer space.

How Sound Bends When sound waves hit a barrier with a small hole in it, some of the waves pass through the hole. Just as diffraction causes water waves to spread out in a harbor, the sound waves spread out, or diffract, as they go through the hole. When sound waves go through a doorway, they spread out. Even if you are off to the side of the room, you may still hear sound from outside. If you are outside the room and not too far from the doorway, you can hear sound coming from inside the room.

Because of diffraction, you can also hear sounds from around corners. Waves passing a corner spread out as they pass.

The Speed of Sound

If you have ever seen a live band perform, you've noticed that the sounds produced by the different instruments and singers all reach your ears at the same time. If they did not travel at the same speed, the sounds that were played together would reach you at different times and would not sound very pleasant.

The speed of sound depends on the properties of the medium it travels through. At room temperature, about 20°C, sound travels at about 340 m/s. This is about twice as fast as most jet airplanes travel through the air. Figure 4 shows the speed of sound through some common materials.

As the properties of a medium change, so too does the speed of the sound that travels through it. **The speed of sound depends on the elasticity, density, and temperature of the medium.**

Elasticity Since sound is a transfer of energy, its speed depends on how well the particles in the medium bounce back after being disturbed. If you stretch a rubber band and then let it go, it returns to its original shape. However, when you stretch modeling clay and then let it go, it stays stretched. Rubber bands are more elastic than modeling clay. **Elasticity** is the ability of a material to bounce back after being disturbed. If a medium is very elastic, its particles easily go back to their original positions. Sound travels more quickly in mediums that have a high degree of elasticity because when the particles are compressed, they quickly spread out again.

Solid materials are usually more elastic than liquids or gases, so compressions and rarefactions travel very well in solids. The particles of a solid do not move very far, so they bounce back and forth quickly as the compressions and rarefactions of the sound waves go by. Most liquids are not very elastic. Sound is not transmitted as well in liquids as it is in solids. Gases are generally very inelastic and are the poorest transmitters of sound.

Density The speed of sound also depends on how close together the particles of the substance are. The **density** of a medium is how much matter, or mass, there is in a given amount of space, or volume.

In materials in the same state of matter—solid, liquid, or gas—sound travels slower in denser mediums. The denser the medium, the more mass it has in a given volume. The particles of a dense material do not move as quickly as those of a less-dense material. Sound travels more slowly in dense metals, such as lead or silver, than in iron or steel.

Temperature In a given medium, sound travels slower at lower temperatures and faster at higher temperatures. At a low temperature, the particles of a medium are more sluggish. They are more difficult to move and return to their original positions more slowly.

At 20°C, the speed of sound in air is about 340 m/s. At 0°C, the speed is about 331 m/s. At higher altitudes the air is colder, so sound travels slower at higher altitudes.

☑ *Checkpoint* *How does elasticity affect the speed of sound?*

Figure 5 Some substances are more elastic than others. Sponges and rubber bands are more elastic than modeling clay. *Predicting Is sound likely to travel faster through a sponge, a rubber band, or a piece of modeling clay?*

Sharpen your Skills

Graphing ACTIVITY

Graph the following data, to show how the speed of sound through air changes with temperature. Show temperature from –20°C to 30°C on the horizontal axis. (*Note:* Negative numbers are less than zero.) Plot speed from 300 m/s to 400 m/s on the vertical axis.

Air Temperature (°C)	Speed (m/s)
–20	318
–10	324
0	330
10	336
20	342
30	348

How does air temperature affect the speed of sound?

Figure 6 On October 14, 1947, Captain Chuck Yeager became the first person to fly a plane faster than the speed of sound (top). On October 15, 1997, Andy Green officially became the first person to drive a land vehicle faster than the speed of sound (bottom).

Moving Faster Than Sound

The supersonic age began with a bang on October 14, 1947. Far above the California desert, Captain Chuck Yeager of the United States Air Force had just "broken the sound barrier." Captain Yeager was at an altitude of 12,000 meters and just about out of fuel. He had used much of his fuel to get higher rather than faster because the speed of sound is less higher up. Wide open throttles accelerated his plane to over 293 meters per second, the speed of sound at that altitude. Thus, when he hit 294 meters per second, he exceeded the speed of sound at that altitude. At a lower altitude, the speed of sound is much higher and he would not have had the power or speed to exceed it. Yeager's team chose to go high because the temperature there is lower and the speed of sound is less. Each pilot today who "goes supersonic" owes Chuck Yeager a debt of gratitude.

Fifty years later, Andy Green stood poised on Nevada's Black Rock desert. He had traveled all the way from Great Britain to go supersonic—on the ground! He chose the desert because it is flat, wide open, and cold in the morning. All of these factors were important to the attempt. On October 15, 1997, at the coolest time of the day, Green blasted off in his jet-powered car, *Thrust*. A short time later he traveled a measured distance at an average speed of 339 meters per second—7 meters per second faster than the speed of sound at that altitude. Andy Green was the first person to break the sound barrier on the ground.

Section 1 Review

1. How does sound travel through a medium?
2. How do elasticity, density, and temperature affect the speed of sound through a medium?
3. Explain why sound cannot travel through outer space.
4. **Thinking Critically Applying Concepts** Sound travels faster through glass than through gold. Based on this information, which material would you say is more dense? Explain.

Science at Home

Find a long metal railing or water pipe. **CAUTION:** *Beware of sharp edges and rust.* Put one ear to the pipe while a family member taps on the pipe some distance away. Do you hear the sound first with the ear touching the pipe or with your other ear? Compare the sound you hear through the metal with the sound coming through the air. What accounts for the difference?

The Speed of Sound

Sound travels at different speeds through different materials. In this lab, you will measure the speed of sound in air.

Problem

How fast does sound travel in air?

Materials (per group of 3)

metric tape measure
drum and drumstick (or empty
   coffee can and metal spoon)
digital stopwatch
thermometer

Procedure

1. With the approval of your teacher, select an outdoor area such as a football field.
2. Record the outdoor air temperature in °C.
3. Measure a distance of 100 meters in a straight line. How long do you think it should take for a sound to travel the 100 m?
4. Stand at one end of this measured distance with the drum. Have two teammates go to the other end with a stopwatch. One teammate, the "watcher," should watch you and the drum. The other, the "listener," should face away from the drum and listen for the sound.
5. Create a short but loud noise by striking the drum.
6. As you strike the drum, the watcher should start the stopwatch. When the listener hears the sound, he or she should immediately say "stop." Then the watcher stops the watch. Record the time to one tenth of a second.
7. Repeat Steps 1–6 five times. How consistent are your times? What accounts for any differences?
8. Now switch roles. Repeat Steps 1–6 with different students beating the drum, watching, and listening.

Analyze and Conclude

1. How far did the sound travel? How long did it take? (Calculate the average of the five measured times.)
2. To calculate the speed of sound in air, use this formula:

$$Speed = \frac{Distance}{Time}$$

3. How well does your result compare with the prediction you made in Step 3? Make a list of reasons for any differences. What could you do to improve the accuracy of your measurements?
4. **Think About It** Another way to measure the speed of sound would be to stand near a tall building, shout, and wait to hear the echo. To use the echo method, what adjustments would you have to make to the procedure in this lab?

Design an Experiment

How could you find out the effect of changing air temperature on the speed of sound? Write a set of procedures you could use to conduct such an experiment.

SECTION 2 Properties of Sound

DISCOVER •••••••••••••••••••••••••••••••••• ACTIVITY

How Does Amplitude Affect Loudness?

1. Your teacher will give you a wooden board with two nails in it. Fasten a guitar string to the board by wrapping each end tightly around a nail.

2. Hold the string near the middle. Pull it about 1 cm to one side. This distance is the amplitude of vibration. Let it go. How far does the string move to the other side? Describe the sound you hear.

3. Repeat Step 2 four more times. Each time, pull the string back a greater distance. Describe how the sound changes each time.

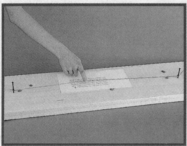

Think It Over

Forming Operational Definitions How would you define the amplitude of the vibration? How did you change the amplitude each time? What effect did changing the amplitude have on the sound?

GUIDE FOR READING

◆ How are sound intensity and loudness related?

◆ How are frequency and pitch related?

◆ What causes the Doppler effect?

Reading Tip As you read, use your own words to write a phrase or sentence describing each boldfaced word.

Suppose you and a friend are standing next to each other. You are talking in your normal speaking voice. After you say good-bye and your friend has walked away, you realize you have forgotten to tell your friend something important. How do you get your friend's attention? You will need to shout to be heard. When you shout, you take a deep breath and exhale very fast, and your voice sounds louder.

Intensity and Loudness

Compare the sound of a whisper to that of a hearty shout. The sounds are different because the amount of energy carried by the sound waves is different. The sound waves caused by a shout carry much more energy than those of a whisper.

Intensity You have seen how you can change the amplitude of a wave along a rope. If you move the rope a greater distance, you give it more energy as you shake it. When a sound wave carries a large amount of energy, the molecules of the medium move a greater distance as the waves pass by, and the sound wave has a greater amplitude. The **intensity** of a sound wave is the amount of energy the wave carries per second through a unit area. Intensity is measured in watts per square meter (W/m^2).

Loudness If you did the Discover activity with the guitar string, you noticed how pulling the string back different distances affected the loudness of the sound you heard. You changed the amplitude of vibration of the string. Sound waves of higher amplitude have a greater intensity because they carry more energy per second through a given area. Though intensity and loudness are not exactly the same, the greater the intensity of a sound wave, the louder it is. **Loudness** describes what you actually hear. **A sound wave of greater intensity sounds louder.**

To increase the loudness of the music coming from a CD player, you adjust the volume control. Loudspeakers or headphones give off sound by vibrating a cone of material. Figure 7 shows how the vibrations make compressions and rarefactions in the air, just like a vibrating drumhead. As you turn up the volume, the cone vibrates with a greater amplitude and the sound you hear is louder.

Loudness, or sound level, is measured in **decibels** (**dB**). Figure 8 shows the loudness of some familiar sounds. The loudness of a sound you can barely hear is about 0 dB. Each 10 dB increase in sound level represents a tenfold increase in intensity. For example, a sound at 30 dB is ten times more intense than a sound at 20 dB. Sounds louder than 100 dB can cause damage to your ears, especially if you listen to those sounds for long periods of time. Sounds louder than 120 dB can cause pain and sometimes permanent hearing loss.

Figure 7 A loudspeaker gives out sound by vibrating cones of material. The greater the amplitude of vibration, the greater the volume, or loudness, of the sound.

✓ *Checkpoint* *How does amplitude affect the loudness of a sound?*

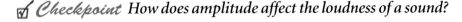

Loudness of Sounds

Sound	Loudness (dB)	Hearing Damage
Threshold of human hearing	0	None
Rustling leaves	10	
Whisper	20	
Very soft music	30	
Classroom	35	
Average home	40–50	
Loud conversation	60–70	
Heavy street traffic	70	
Loud music	90–100	After long exposure
Subway train	100	
Rock concert	115–120	Progressive
Jackhammer	120	Threshold of pain
Jet engine	120–170	
Space shuttle engine	200	Immediate and irreversible

Figure 8 Some sounds are so soft, you can barely hear them. Others are so loud that they can damage your ears. *Applying Concepts How is the sound of a space shuttle engine different from that of a whisper?*

The Short Straw

Try this activity **ACTIVITY** to see how the length of a straw affects the sound it makes when you blow through it.

1. Flatten one end of a drinking straw and cut the end to form a point.
2. Blow through the straw. Describe what you hear.

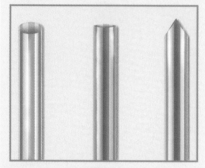

Predicting What changes would you hear if you shortened the straw by cutting off some of the straight end? Test your prediction.

Frequency and Pitch

A barbershop quartet consists of four singers with very different voices. When all four people sing together, the different voices combine to make a pleasing sound.

Frequency When a person sings, muscles in the throat stretch and relax the vocal cords. This changes the frequency of the sounds. When the vocal cords are stretched, they vibrate more often as the air rushes past them. This creates higher-frequency sound waves. When the vocal cords are relaxed, they vibrate less often and produce lower-frequency sound waves. The frequency of a sound wave is the number of vibrations that occur per second. A frequency of 50 Hz means fifty vibrations per second. A bass singer can produce a range of frequencies from about 80 Hz to about 260 Hz. A trained soprano voice can produce frequencies over 1,000 Hz.

Most people can hear sounds with frequencies between 20 Hz and 20,000 Hz. Sound waves with frequencies above the normal human range of hearing are called **ultrasound**. The prefix *ultra-* means "above." Sounds with frequencies below the normal human range of hearing are called **infrasound**. The prefix *infra-* means "below."

Pitch Before a barbershop quartet begins to sing, one member plays a note on a pitch pipe. This gives the lead singer the correct starting note. The **pitch** of a sound is a description of how high or low the sound seems to a person. **The pitch of a sound that you hear depends on the frequency of the sound wave.** Sound waves of high frequency have a high pitch, while sound waves of low frequency have a low pitch.

Figure 9 A barbershop quartet consists of four singers, whose voices sound good together. *Comparing and Contrasting In what way are the four voices different?*

Figure 10 The key farthest to the left on a piano is attached to the longest string. This key plays the note with the lowest pitch.
Developing Hypotheses Why do longer strings generally produce lower notes than shorter ones?

When a string vibrates, the pitch of the sound depends on the material used, the length and thickness of the string, and on how tightly it is stretched. You can change the pitch of a sound by changing the properties of the string that produces it. For example, violinists and guitarists tune their instruments by turning knobs that stretch the strings. A tighter string produces a higher frequency. You hear the higher frequency as a sound with higher pitch.

Different lengths of string produce different frequencies, too. In general, a short string produces a higher pitch than a long string under the same tension. Consider the range of notes you can play on a piano. The key farthest to the left on a piano keyboard produces the note with the lowest pitch. It is attached to the longest string, which vibrates at a frequency of about 27 Hz. The key farthest to the right on a piano keyboard produces the note with the highest pitch. It is attached to the shortest string, which vibrates at a frequency of about 4,186 Hz.

☑ *Checkpoint* *How are frequency and pitch related?*

Resonance Have you ever heard of an opera singer who could shatter a glass with a sustained high note? How can that happen? All objects vibrate naturally. The vibrations are so frequent that you usually cannot see them. The frequency of the vibrations depends on the type and shape of the object. If the frequency of sound waves exactly matches the natural frequency of an object, the sound waves can add to the object's vibrations. Resonance occurs when the frequency of the sound waves and the natural frequency of the object are the same.

Suppose a note has the same frequency as the natural vibration of a crystal glass. If the note is played steadily, the sound waves can add to the amplitude of vibration of the glass. If the note is played loudly enough and for long enough, the amplitude of vibration can increase so much that the glass shatters.

Figure 11 Some musical instruments can produce notes with vibrations that match the natural frequency of a crystal glass. If the note is sustained, the amplitude of vibration can cause the glass to shatter.

The Doppler Effect

Even though a sound may have a constant frequency, it does not always sound that way to a listener. Have you ever heard a police car speed by with its siren on? If you listen carefully you will notice something surprising. As the car moves toward you, the pitch of the siren is higher. As the car goes by and moves away, the pitch drops. But the frequency of the siren is not really changing. If you were riding in the police car, you would hear the same pitch all the time. The apparent change in frequency as a wave source moves in relation to the listener is called the **Doppler effect.** If the waves are sound waves, the change in frequency is heard as a change in pitch.

The Doppler Demonstration The Doppler effect was named after Christian Doppler, an Austrian scientist who described it about 150 years ago. To demonstrate the effect, Doppler put a musical band on an open flatcar of a train. He stood on the ground nearby. As the train approached him, the notes the musicians played seemed to be a higher pitch. As the train passed, the notes seemed to drop in pitch. Doppler repeated the experiment, but this time he stood on the train and had the musicians play while they were seated on the ground. Doppler heard the same changes in pitch as the train he rode approached and passed the band. The effect was the same regardless of who was moving, the band or Doppler.

Changing Pitch To understand what causes this apparent change in pitch, imagine you are standing still and throwing tennis balls at a wall about 5 meters in front of you. If you throw one ball each second, the balls hit the wall at a rate of one per second. The frequency is 1 per second, or 1 Hz. Now suppose you walk toward the wall, still throwing one ball per second.

Figure 12 As the police car speeds by, the pitch of the siren seems to change. Ahead of the car, the sound waves are piling up, so the pitch is higher. Behind the car the waves spread out, so the pitch is lower.

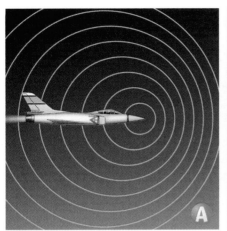
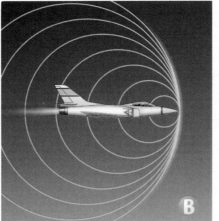
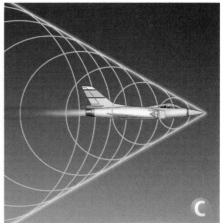

Figure 13 When a plane flies faster than the speed of sound, it breaks through a pile-up of waves known as the sound barrier.

Because each ball has a shorter distance to travel than the one before, it takes less time to get there. The balls hit the wall more often than one per second, or with a higher frequency than before. Similarly, if you throw balls at the wall as you back away, the balls will hit the wall with lower frequency. Each ball has farther to travel before it hits the wall, so it takes longer to get there.

Figure 12 shows how sound waves from a moving source behave. **As a sound source moves toward the listener, the waves reach the listener with a higher frequency. The pitch appears to increase because of the Doppler effect.**

This piling up of sound waves has a spectacular effect in the air. Figures 13A and B show how as a plane travels almost as fast as the speed of sound, the sound waves pile up in front of the plane. This pile-up is the "sound barrier." When the plane flies faster than the speed of sound, it breaks through the barrier. When the sound barrier is broken, as in Figure 13C, it releases a huge amount of energy in the form of a shock wave. People on the ground nearby hear a loud noise called a sonic boom.

Section 2 Review

1. What makes some sounds louder than others?
2. Explain the relationship between frequency and pitch.
3. How can you change the pitch produced by a vibrating string?
4. Explain how resonance can cause a crystal glass to shatter.
5. What is the Doppler effect?
6. **Thinking Critically Relating Cause and Effect** If you are riding in a fire truck with the siren blaring, you do not hear the Doppler effect. Explain.

Check Your Progress

CHAPTER PROJECT 2

Think about the design of your instrument and how it will produce sounds. Consider how you will vary the sound produced by your instrument. Make a list of the materials you could use to build your instrument. Begin to collect your materials.

SECTION 3 Combining Sound Waves

DISCOVER •••••••••••••••••••••••••••••••••••• ACTIVITY

How Can You Produce Patterns of Sound?

1. Obtain an empty coffee can.

2. Stretch the palm area of a latex glove over the open end. Glue a small mirror tile in the center of the glove.

3. Shine a flashlight so that the light reflects off the mirror and onto a wall.

4. Ask a classmate to continuously tap a spoon on the closed end of the can. Make sure you keep the light shining on the mirror. Observe the light patterns that are reflected on the wall. What do the patterns look like? Draw and label what you observe.

5. Have your classmate change the frequency of the tapping. Draw what you observe.

Think It Over
Inferring What causes the moving patterns on the wall? What happens when you change the frequency of the tapping? Explain.

GUIDE FOR READING

◆ What is sound quality?

◆ How are music and noise different?

◆ What happens when two or more sound waves interact?

Reading Tip Before you read, list as many musical instruments as you can. Write a short description of how you think each one works. Revise your list as you read.

Imagine you are waiting for a train at a busy station. In the middle of all the hustle and bustle, you notice lots of different sounds. A baby wails while a teenager listens to a favorite radio station. Then the train rolls in. Why are some sounds pleasing to hear while others make you want to cover your ears? The answer is in the way sound waves combine.

Busy train station ▶

Sound Quality

Think of all the different sounds you hear on a given day. Some sounds are pleasant, such as your favorite kind of music, a babbling brook, or a baby cooing. Other sounds are unpleasant, such as loud power tools, fingernails scratching on a chalkboard, or a constant drip of water from a tap. Your ears hear all kinds of sounds—some that you like and some that you don't.

To understand the quality of sound, consider the example of a violin string. As the string vibrates, waves travel along the string and then reflect back, setting up a standing wave. Figure 14 shows how a string vibrates with different frequencies. The frequency at which a standing wave occurs is the string's resonant frequency. Every object, including musical instruments, has its own resonant frequency.

The resonant frequency produces a pitch called the fundamental, or pure, tone. However, most of the sounds you hear are not pure tones. Although a tuning fork or pitch pipe produces a single tone, more complex instruments produce several tones at once. For example, as a whole string vibrates at one frequency, sections of the string vibrate at a higher frequency. These vibrations produce sounds with higher pitch. The higher pitches, or overtones, have frequencies of two, three, or four times the frequency of the fundamental tone.

Timbre (TAM bur) describes the quality of the sound you hear. Overtones can be weak, strong, or missing. The timbre of a sound depends on which overtones are present.

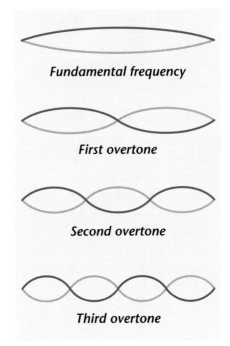

Fundamental frequency

First overtone

Second overtone

Third overtone

Figure 14 When the whole string vibrates, it produces a fundamental tone (top). When some sections of the string vibrate faster than other parts, overtones are produced. *Inferring How does the pitch of each overtone compare with the pitch of the fundamental tone?*

The blending of the fundamental tone and the overtones makes up the characteristic sound quality, or timbre, of a particular sound.

Sounds produced by different instruments have different timbres. The sound of a note played on a trumpet has a different timbre from the same note played on a violin or flute. The trumpet, the violin, and the flute produce different overtones. The size, shape, and materials used also affect the timbre of an instrument.

✓ *Checkpoint* **What factors affect the quality of a sound?**

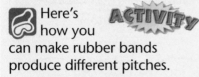
Making Music

If the combination of the fundamental tone and the overtones results in a sound with a pleasing timbre and a clear pitch, the sound is considered **music.** Most music contains only a few fundamental tones and their overtones. **Music is a set of tones combined in ways that are pleasing to the ear.** The design of a musical instrument affects the overtones it produces when a note is played. All musical instruments produce vibrations when played. The material that vibrates varies. The major groups of instruments are strings, brass, woodwinds, and percussion.

Strings Stringed instruments have strings that vibrate when plucked, struck, or rubbed with a bow. A short string vibrates at a higher frequency and so produces a higher-pitched sound than a long string. As they play, musicians place their fingers on different places along the string to vary the pitch. The material, thickness, and tightness of a string also affects the pitch it produces. Instruments such as guitars, violins, and cellos also have a box, or sounding board. The box improves the quality of the sound produced by the strings. Larger stringed instruments, such as the cello and the double bass, produce lower pitches.

Brass and Woodwinds Brass instruments, such as trumpets and trombones, produce sound when the player's lips vibrate against the mouthpiece. This vibration causes the air column inside the instrument to vibrate. The musician adjusts the length of the air column by pressing valves or moving slides.

Figure 15 Violins are stringed instruments, flutes and clarinets are woodwinds, and trumpets are brass instruments.
Making Generalizations What do all these musical instruments have in common?

Many woodwind instruments, such as clarinets and oboes, have a thin, flexible strip of material called a reed. When the player blows into the mouthpiece, the reed vibrates along with the column of air. The longer the column of air, the lower the pitch. Larger woodwind and brass instruments, such as the bassoon and the tuba, produce lower pitches.

Percussion Percussion instruments, such as drums, bells, cymbals, and xylophones, vibrate when struck. The sound they produce depends on the material from which they are made. It also depends on the size of the instrument, and the part of the instrument that is played. For example, larger drums produce lower pitches.

Figure 16 Percussion instruments vibrate when struck. *Predicting Describe the sound produced by a large drum compared with that of a small drum of the same material.*

✓ *Checkpoint* *What are the main groups of musical instruments?*

Noise

You are sitting comfortably in your classroom chair, watching a classmate write on the board. Suddenly, you hear the accidental scratch of fingernails as the chalk flies from your friend's grasp. The sound makes you wince.

Why is the squeak of fingernails on a chalkboard so unpleasant? One answer is that the squeak is noise. **Noise** is a mixture of sound waves that do not sound pleasing together. **Noise has no pleasing timbre and no identifiable pitch.** Consider the noise of chalk squeaking on a chalkboard or the noise of a jackhammer working in the street. The vibrations that produce these sounds are random. Even if an engine produces a hum that has a fundamental tone and overtones, the lack of rhythm in the sound makes us call it noise instead of music.

Sounds that are music to some people are noise to others. Some rock bands and orchestras play compositions with tones that seem to have no musical relationship. The sound produced when these notes are played together is called **dissonance.** Dissonance is music to the ears of people who enjoy the sound.

Music CONNECTION

One of the most widely known compositions of Sergei Prokofiev, a Russian composer who lived from 1891 to 1953, is *Peter and the Wolf*. In this work, each instrument, or group of instruments, represents a character in the story.

In Your Journal

Listen to a recording of *Peter and the Wolf*. Write a review of this work. Do you agree with how Prokofiev matched instruments with characters? Which instrument would you have chosen to represent each character?

EXPLORING *Making Music*

The sound produced by a musical instrument depends on the instrument's size and shape. The material from which the instrument is made and the way it is played also affect the timbre of the sound.

Violin
The violin is a carefully crafted wooden box with strings. The strings are attached to tuning pegs, which can be turned to adjust the tension. When the strings are rubbed with a bow, they vibrate. The violinist controls the pitch by placing the fingers at different positions along the string.

Harp
The harp consists of a row of strings, each one a different length. The harpist gracefully plucks the strings with the fingers to produce music. The short strings produce higher pitches than the long strings do.

Clarinet
The clarinet is a woodwind instrument. It has a single reed that vibrates when the player blows into the mouthpiece. The vibrations set up resonance in the air column. The player changes the pitch by pressing on the keys.

Electronic Keyboard
A keyboard is a common name for an electronic music maker. It uses a computer chip to reproduce the sound of many different instruments by matching the tones and overtones that the individual instruments produce.

French Horn
The French horn is a brass instrument. When the musician's lips vibrate in the mouthpiece, the 2 m-long column of air vibrates. The player changes the length of the air column by pressing and releasing keys. This changes the pitch of the notes produced.

Interference of Sound Waves

You have probably heard sound waves interfering with each other, though you may not have known what you were hearing. **Interference occurs when two or more sound waves interact.** The amplitudes of the two waves combine, causing the loudness of the sound to change. When interference is constructive, compressions of waves occur at the same place and the amplitudes combine. The resulting sound is louder than either of the two original sounds. When the interference is destructive, compressions of one wave occur at the same place as rarefactions of another wave and the amplitudes cancel each other out. The resulting wave is softer or completely concealed.

Figure 17 A concert hall must be designed to provide the highest sound quality possible. The design should eliminate echoes and destructive interference.

Acoustics The way in which sound waves interact is very important in concert halls. In a concert hall, sound waves of different frequencies reach each listener from many directions at the same time. These sound waves may come directly from the orchestra or they may first bounce off the walls or ceiling. People sitting in various seats may hear different sounds because of the particular interactions of sound waves at their locations. In a poorly designed hall, seats may be located where destructive interference occurs. The sound will seem distorted.

Acoustics describe how well sounds can be heard in a particular room or hall. When designing auditoriums, acoustical engineers must carefully consider the shape of the room and the materials used to cover walls, floors, ceilings, and seats. Because they absorb sound instead of reflecting it, some materials can eliminate the reflected waves that cause inference.

Canceling Sounds Sometimes destructive interference is welcome.

INTEGRATING TECHNOLOGY Airplane passengers use earphones to listen to music, but the throbbing of the plane's engines can drown out much of the sound. Some airline earphones use destructive interference to cancel out the steady engine noise. The earphones produce sound waves that interfere destructively with the engine sound. The passenger's ears receive both the engine sound waves and the sound waves produced by the earphones. These waves cancel each other out, so the passenger hears neither. Only the music is left. This type of technology also allows factories to reduce noise levels to protect the hearing of workers.

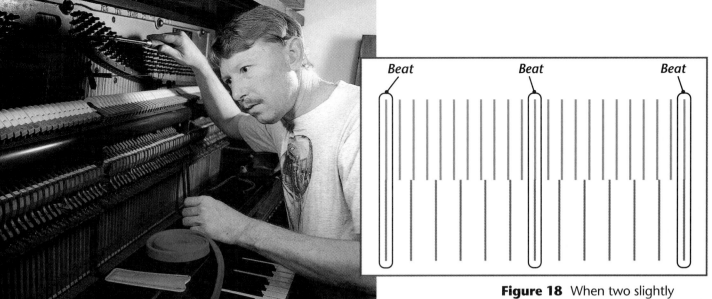

Figure 18 When two slightly different frequencies are combined, they interfere constructively at regular intervals (above right). A piano tuner listens to the sound of a note and a tuning fork together (above left). *Inferring How does the piano tuner know when a key is perfectly tuned?*

Beats If two sound waves are close in frequency, they can combine so that they interfere both constructively and destructively at regular intervals. Figure 18 shows how two frequencies can combine at certain times. The resulting sound gets louder and softer at regular intervals. The intervals depend on the difference between the two frequencies. The repeated changes in loudness are called **beats.**

Piano tuners use beats to tune pianos. A piano tuner strikes a tuning fork of a particular frequency and hits the corresponding key on a piano at the same time. If the tuner hears beats, that means that the frequency of vibration of the piano string does not exactly match that of the tuning fork. The tuner then adjusts the piano string until no beat can be heard. Then the piano key is perfectly tuned.

Section 3 Review

1. What factors determine the quality of a sound?
2. What is the difference between music and noise?
3. How can sounds cancel each other out?
4. How can the interference of two sound waves produce a louder sound?
5. What are beats?
6. **Thinking Critically** **Applying Concepts** Explain why a sound in an empty room will sound different from the same sound in a room with a carpet, curtains, and furniture.

Check Your Progress .... CHAPTER PROJECT 2
Begin building the instrument you have designed. As you build your instrument, experiment with different materials to find the most appealing sound. How do different kinds of materials affect the sounds? Explore and experiment with the sounds your instrument makes. How does adding or removing certain parts or materials affect the loudness of the sound? How can you vary the pitch of your instrument?

Real-World Lab

Musical Notes

usical instruments produce sound by setting up standing waves. Those waves can be on a string or in a column of air. In this lab, you will see how you can use bottles to produce different musical notes, maybe enough to play a simple tune.

Problem

How can you produce different notes with bottles of water?

Skills Focus

predicting, observing, inferring

Materials

3 identical glass bottles
water
masking tape
marking pen
pencil

Procedure

1. Label the bottles A, B, and C.
2. Put water in each bottle so that bottle A is one-fourth full, bottle B is half full, and bottle C is three-fourths full.
3. Copy the data table into your lab notebook. Measure the distance from the top of each bottle to the surface of the water. Then measure the height of the water in each bottle. Record your measurements.
4. Predict the difference in pitch you will hear if you blow across the top of each bottle in turn. Give reasons for your prediction.
5. Test your prediction by blowing over the top of each bottle. Listen to the sound you produce. Describe each sound in terms of its pitch— low, medium, or high. Record the pitch of each sound.

DATA TABLE

Bottle	Length of Column of Air (cm)	Height of Water (cm)	Pitch Produced by Blowing Across Top of Bottle	Pitch Produced by Tapping Pencil on Side of Bottle
A				
B				
C				

5. Compare the sounds you produced by blowing across the bottles with those produced by tapping on the bottles. What was the difference in pitch for each bottle? Explain your observations.

6. Look at your data table. How does the length of the column of air affect the pitch? How does the height of the water affect the pitch?

7. **Think About It** Based on your observations in this lab, what statements can you make about the relationship between the sounds produced and the medium through which the sound travels?

More to Explore

To play simple tunes, you will need eight notes. Set up a row of eight bottles, each with a different amount of water. Adjust the water level in each bottle until you can play a simple scale. Practice playing a simple tune on your bottles.

6. When you gently tap the side of a bottle with a pencil, you produce another sound. Do you think the sound will be similar to or different from the sound produced by blowing across the top of the bottle? Explain.

7. Test your prediction by tapping on the side of each bottle with a pencil. Record the pitch of each sound.

Analyze and Conclude

1. Describe how the sound is produced in Step 5. Which bottle produced the highest pitch? Which bottle produced the lowest pitch?

2. What caused the change in pitch from bottle to bottle?

3. Describe how the sound is produced in Step 7. Which bottle produced the highest pitch? Which bottle produced the lowest pitch?

4. What caused the change in pitch from bottle to bottle? What change in pitch can you produce by tapping on a different part of the bottle?

SECTION 4 How You Hear Sound

Where Is the Sound Coming From?

1. Ask your partner to sit on a chair, with eyes closed.

2. Clap your hands near your partner's left ear. Ask your partner to tell you the direction the sound came from.

3. Now clap near your partner's right ear. Again, ask your partner to tell you the direction the sound came from. Continue clapping above your partner's head, in front of the face, and below the chin in random order. How well can your partner detect the direction the sound is coming from?

4. Switch places with your partner and repeat Steps 1–3.

Think It Over

Observing As you clap, record the answers given by your partner. Which locations are easily identified? Which locations were impossible to identify? Is there a pattern? If so, can you think of a possible explanation for this pattern?

GUIDE FOR READING

◆ How do you hear sound?

◆ What causes hearing loss?

Reading Tip As you read, draw a flowchart to show how you hear sound.

The house is quiet. You are sound asleep. All of a sudden, your alarm clock goes off. Startled, you jump up out of bed. Your ears detected the sound waves produced by the alarm clock. But how exactly did your brain receive the information?

How You Hear Sound

Once the sound waves enter your ear, how does your brain receive the information? Your ear has three main sections: the outer ear, the middle ear, and the inner ear. Each has a different function. **The outer ear funnels sound waves, the middle ear transmits the waves inward, and the inner ear converts the sound waves into a form that your brain can understand.**

Outer Ear As the alarm clock rings, the sound waves reach your ears. The curved surface of the outermost part of your ear looks and acts like a funnel. It collects sound waves and directs them into a narrower region known as the **ear canal.** Your ear

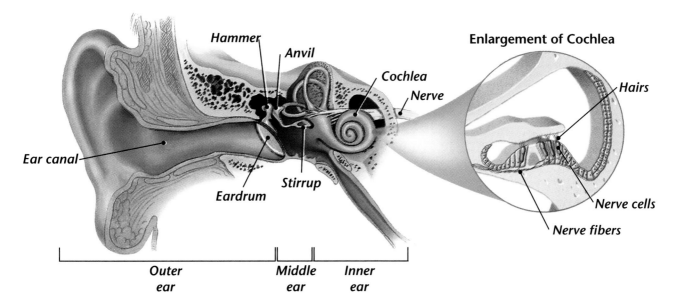

Hammer
Anvil
Cochlea
Nerve
Ear canal
Stirrup
Eardrum

Outer
ear

Middle
ear

Inner
ear

Enlargement of Cochlea

Hairs
Nerve cells
Nerve fibers

Figure 19 The illustrations show the structure of the human ear and the inside of the cochlea.
Interpreting Diagrams How is sound transmitted through the middle ear?

canal is a few centimeters long and ends at the eardrum. The **eardrum** is a small, tightly stretched, drumlike membrane. The sound waves make your eardrum vibrate, just as a drum vibrates when you beat it with a drumstick.

Middle Ear Behind the eardrum is an area called the middle ear. The **middle ear** contains the three smallest bones in the human body—the hammer, the anvil, and the stirrup. If you look at them in Figure 19, you'll see how they got their names. The hammer is attached to the eardrum, so when the eardrum vibrates, the hammer does too. The hammer then hits the anvil, which then shakes the stirrup.

Inner Ear The inner ear is separated from the middle ear by another membrane. Behind this membrane is a cavity filled with liquid. This cavity, the **cochlea** (KAHK lee uh), is shaped like a snail shell. Inside, it is lined with more than 10,000 tiny hairs. When the stirrup vibrates against the membrane, the vibrations pass into the liquid in the cochlea. As the liquid moves, the hairs sway back and forth. The hairs are attached to nerve cells that detect this movement. Nerve fibers send messages to the brain. The brain processes these messages and tells you that you've heard sound.

☑ *Checkpoint* **What are the three main areas of the ear?**

Listen to Sounds

How does sound travel to your ears?

1. Tie two strings to the handle of a metal spoon. Each string should be about 40 cm long.
2. Hold one end of each string in each hand. Bump the bowl of the spoon against a desk or other hard solid object. Listen to the sound.
3. Now wrap the ends of the string around your fingers.
4. Put your index fingers up against your ears and bump the spoon against the object again.

Inferring How does the first sound compare with the sound you heard with your fingers up against your ears? What can you conclude about how sound travels to your ears?

Hearing Loss

Figure 20 Hearing aids can make sounds louder as the sounds enter the ear.

 INTEGRATING HEALTH The human ear can normally detect sounds as soft as breathing (about 2–10 dB). The normal range of frequencies a person can hear is 20–20,000 Hz. However, when hearing loss occurs, a person may have difficulty hearing very soft sounds or high pitches. **Many people suffer hearing loss as a result of injury, infection, or aging.**

Hearing Loss Due to Injury or Infection A head injury can cause the tiny hammer, anvil, and stirrup to disconnect from each other. When this happens, sound cannot be transmitted through the middle ear. Surgery can usually correct this type of hearing loss.

If your eardrum becomes damaged or punctured, you may experience hearing loss. (Imagine trying to play a torn drum!) For this reason, it is dangerous to put objects into your ear, even to clean it. Viral or bacterial infections can also damage the delicate inner ear, causing permanent hearing loss.

Hearing Loss Due to Aging The most common type of hearing loss occurs gradually as people age. As a person gets older, the tiny hairs in the cochlea become less effective at detecting the signals. Many older people cannot hear higher-frequency sounds.

Extended exposure to loud sounds can kill the hairs too. If the hairs are damaged by loud sounds, they can no longer transmit signals to the brain. You can prevent this type of hearing loss by wearing ear plugs or other hearing protection when you know you are going to be exposed to loud noises.

Some types of hearing loss can be helped using hearing aids. Most hearing aids make sounds louder by using the ear canal and the eardrum as amplifiers. Others are surgically attached to the anvil, causing it to vibrate more than usual when a sound enters the ear. Some hearing aids are so tiny that they can fit invisibly into your ear canal.

Section 4 Review

1. How do your ears detect sound waves?
2. How can sound damage your hearing?
3. Describe how the eardrum works.
4. What happens once sound waves enter the ear?
5. **Thinking Critically Classifying** Make a chart that lists some common sounds you might hear in a day. Estimate the loudness of each sound and state whether each one could produce hearing loss. (*Hint:* Refer to Figure 8 on page 47.)

Science at Home

Invite family members to make a survey of the kinds of sounds they hear throughout one day. Have each member rate the sounds as quiet, normal, loud, or painful. Then rate each sound as pleasant, neutral, or annoying. State the source of each sound, the location, the time of day, and the approximate length of time that they are exposed to the sound. How are the ratings alike and different?

Keeping It Quiet...

A construction worker operates a jackhammer; a woman waits in a noisy subway station; a factory worker uses loud machinery. All three are victims of noise pollution. In the United States, 80 million people say they are "continually" bothered by noise, and 40 million face danger to their health.

One burst of sound from a passing truck can be enough to raise blood pressure. People start to feel pain at about 120 decibels. Exposure to even 85 decibels (the noise level of a kitchen blender or a loudly crying baby) can eventually damage the hairs of the cochlea. Noise that "doesn't hurt" can still damage your hearing. As many as 16 million Americans may have permanent hearing loss caused by noise. What can we do to keep it quiet?

The Issues

What Can Individual People Do? Some work conditions are noisier than others. Construction workers, factory employees, and people who drive large vehicles are often at risk. All workers in noisy environments can benefit from ear protectors, such as plugs or headphone-like mufflers. Ear protectors can reduce noise levels by 35 decibels.

A listener at a rock concert, a hunter firing a rifle, or someone using an electric drill can also prevent damage with ear protectors. In addition, people should, if possible, avoid extreme noise. They can buy quieter machines and respect neighbors by not using noisy machines, such as lawn mowers and snow blowers, at quiet times of day or night. Simply turning down the volume on headphones, radios, CD players, and tape players can prevent one of the most frequent causes of permanent hearing loss in young people.

What Can Communities Do?
Transportation—planes, trains, trucks, and cars— is the largest source of noise pollution. Fifteen million Americans live near airports or under airport flight paths. Careful planning to locate highways and airports away from homes and buildings can reduce noise. Cities and towns can also prohibit flights late at night.

Many communities have laws against noise of more than a fixed decibel level, but these laws are not always enforced. In some cities "noise police" can fine the owners of noisy equipment.

What Can Government Do? A national Office of Noise Abatement and Control was set up in the 1970s. It required labels on power tools and lawnmowers telling how much noise they make. In 1982, this office was closed down. Some lawmakers want to bring the office back and have nationwide limits to many types of noise. But critics say that national laws have little effect in controlling noise. The federal government could also encourage—and pay for—research into making quieter vehicles and machines.

You Decide

1. **Identify the Problem**
   In your own words, describe the problem of noise pollution.

2. **Analyze the Options**
   List as many methods as you can for dealing with noise. How would each method work to reduce noise or to protect people from noise? Who would be affected by each method?

3. **Find a Solution**
   Propose one method for reducing noise in your community. Make a poster that encourages people to carry out your proposal.

SECTION
5

DISCOVER • **ACTIVITY** • • • •

How Can You Use Time to Measure Distance?

1. Measure a distance 3 meters from a wall and mark the spot with a piece of masking tape.

2. Roll a soft ball in a straight line from that spot toward the wall. What happens to the ball?

3. Roll the ball again. Try to roll the ball at the same speed each time. Have a classmate use a stopwatch to record the time it takes for the ball to leave your hand, reflect off the wall, and then return to you.

4. Now move 6 meters away from the wall. Mark the spot with tape. Repeat Steps 2 and 3.

5. Compare the time for both distances.

Think It Over

Inferring What does the difference in time tell you about the distance the ball has traveled?

GUIDE FOR READING

◆ How is sonar used to tell distances?

◆ How do animals use sound?

◆ How is ultrasound used in medicine?

Reading Tip As you read, write a sentence or two that describes each application of sound waves.

You and your friend are in a long, dark cave. Every sound you make seems to come right back to you. For fun, both of you shout and scream and then listen as the echoes bounce around the cave.

Reflection of Sound Waves

When a sound wave hits a surface through which it cannot pass, it bounces back, or reflects. A reflected sound wave is called an echo.

Sometimes an echo is much fainter than the original sound. This is usually because some of the energy of the wave is absorbed along the way. Some materials reflect sound very well, while others absorb most of the sound that strikes them. Most of the practical applications of sound are based on the fact that sound reflects off some surfaces.

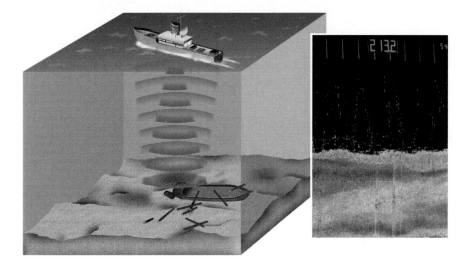

Figure 21 Sonar is used to determine distances and to locate objects under water. *Applying Concepts What two quantities must be known to calculate how far a sound wave has traveled?*

Sonar

Reflected sound waves have many uses. They can be used to determine the depth of water, to locate a sunken shipwreck or cargo, to find schools of fish, or to locate boats out on the ocean.

Sonar is a system of detecting reflected sound waves. The word *sonar* comes from the initial letters of **so**und **n**avigation **a**nd **r**anging. "Navigation" means finding your way around on the ocean (or in the air), and "ranging" means finding the distance between objects. Submarines and ships use sonar to detect other submarines and ships by sending sound waves through the water close to the surface. When the waves hit another boat near the surface of the water, they reflect back and are picked up by the sonar device.

How Sonar Works A sonar machine, or depth finder, produces a burst of high-frequency ultrasonic sound waves that travels through the water. When the waves hit an object or the ocean floor, they reflect. The reflected waves are detected by the sonar machine. **The sonar device measures the time it takes to detect the reflected sound waves.** It uses the data to calculate the distance that the sound has traveled. The intensity of the reflected waves tells the size and shape of the object that reflected the waves.

Calculating Distances The farther a sound wave travels before bouncing off a barrier, the longer it takes to come back. To calculate the depth of water, the sonar machine must calculate the distance traveled by the sound waves. It measures the time taken for the waves to come back. The sonar device then multiplies the speed of sound in water by the time taken. The total distance traveled by the sound is twice the depth of the water. Because the waves traveled to the bottom and then back, the sonar machine divides the total distance by two to find the actual depth.

Checkpoint *What are three uses for sonar?*

Sharpen your Skills

Designing Experiments

ACTIVITY

1. Stand a square piece of cardboard on a table. Prop it up with a book.

2. Put two empty paper towel or aluminum foil tubes on the table. The tubes should be at an angle to each other and almost touching at the end near the cardboard. Leave a gap of about 6 cm between the cardboard and the ends of the tubes.

3. Put your ear near the other end of one of the tubes. Cover one ear with your hand so that the only sounds you hear are coming through the tube.

4. Place a ticking watch in the second tube and cover the open end with your hand. What do you hear?

5. Design an experiment to determine how sound reflects off different materials, such as a variety of fabrics.

Figure 22 Elephants communicate using low-frequency, or infrasonic, sound waves.

Uses of Ultrasound and Infrasound

The dog trainer stands quietly, watching the dog a short distance away. To get the dog's attention, the trainer blows into a small whistle. You don't hear a thing. But the dog stops, cocks an ear, and then comes running toward the trainer. What did the dog hear that you didn't? Dogs can hear ultrasonic frequencies of over 20,000 Hz, well above the upper limit for humans.

Some animals communicate using sounds with frequencies that humans cannot hear. When elephants get upset, they stomp on the ground. The stomping produces low-frequency, or infrasonic, sound waves—too low for humans to hear. The waves travel through the ground for distances of up to 50 kilometers and can be detected by other elephants.

Ultrasound in the Ocean Dolphins and whales emit pings of

INTEGRATING LIFE SCIENCE

sound at frequencies that are high, but not too high for you to hear. **Echolocation** (ek oh loh KAY shun) is the use of sound waves to determine distances or to locate objects. Dolphins and whales use echolocation to find their way in the ocean, and to find their prey.

It was once thought that fish couldn't hear the high frequencies that dolphins and whales emit. But scientists have discovered that shad, herring, and some other fish can hear sounds as high as 180,000 Hz, nine times as high as the highest frequency you can hear. The fish may use this ability to avoid being eaten by dolphins and whales.

Because sound waves travel so well in water, ultrasound has many uses in the sea. Some fisherman attach ultrasonic beepers to their nets. The ultrasound annoys the dolphins, who then swim away from the nets and do not get caught. Other devices can protect divers from sharks by surrounding the divers with ultrasonic waves that keep sharks away.

Figure 23 Dolphins emit high-frequency sounds to communicate with each other, to navigate, and to find food.

Echolocation in Bats Imagine walking around in a totally dark room. You would bump into the walls and furniture quite often. Bats, however, can fly around dark areas and not bump into anything. **Bats use echolocation to navigate and to find food.**

As bats fly, they send out pulses of sound at frequencies of about 100,000 Hz. Then they listen to how long the sound takes to return. By picking up the reflections, or echoes, a bat can tell if it is about to bump into something. Though bats are not blind, they tend to rely more on their hearing than on their vision to "see" where they are going. Echolocation also tells the bat where its prey is. Bats can use echolocation to hunt. Most bats hunt insects, but some hunt small animals such as mice, rats, frogs, or birds.

Figure 24 Bats use echolocation to locate food and to avoid bumping into objects.

Ultrasound in Medicine Ultrasound allows doctors to get a

![INTEGRATING HEALTH] picture, called a **sonogram,** of the inside of the human body. **Doctors use ultrasound to look inside the human body and to diagnose and treat medical conditions.**

To examine a pregnant woman, the doctor holds a small probe on the woman's abdomen. The probe generates very high-frequency sound waves (about 2 million Hz). The ultrasound device detects and measures the ultrasonic waves that bounce back. By analysing the intensity and frequency of the reflected waves, the device builds up a picture. The sonogram can show the position of the developing baby. Sonograms can also show if more than one baby is to be born. In addition to a still picture, an ultrasound can produce a video of a developing baby in motion.

Because of their high frequency, carefully focused ultrasound waves can also painlessly destroy unwanted tissues. In many cases ultrasound can eliminate the need for surgery.

Figure 25 A doctor examines a pregnant woman with an ultrasound machine. A picture of the developing baby is displayed on a screen.

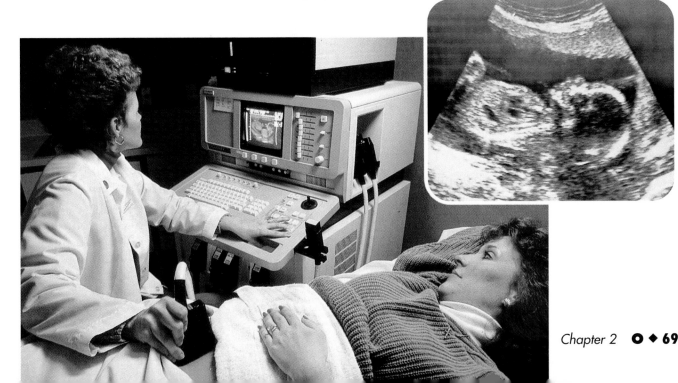

Figure 26 Some examples of common household objects that use ultrasound include an automatic focus camera, an ultrasonic toothbrush, and an ultrasonic jewelry cleaner.

Ultrasound at Home As technology progresses, more and more everyday objects use ultrasonic waves. Imagine cleaning your teeth with sound! If you have used one of the newer electric toothbrushes, you have done just that. The toothbrush sends out high-frequency sound waves that can reach into places that the bristles of the brush cannot.

Ultrasonic jewelry cleaners can clean delicate pieces of jewelry that might be damaged by brushes or harsh detergents. The tub is filled with water and a mild detergent. When the cleaner is switched on, the sound waves move through the water. When they reach the jewelry, the vibrations shake the dirt away, without causing scratches or other damage.

Some cameras use ultrasound to focus automatically. You look through the viewfinder at the object to be photographed. As you push the button to take a picture, the camera sends out ultrasonic waves that reflect off the object and travel back to the camera. The camera measures the time taken for the waves to come back, just like a sonar machine. The camera then calculates the distance to the object and adjusts the lens accordingly.

Section 5 Review

1. What is sonar?
2. How do animals use ultrasound and infrasound?
3. How is ultrasound used in medicine?
4. What household devices use sound waves? What is the function of sound in each device?
5. **Thinking Critically** **Calculating** The speed of sound in ocean water is about 1,530 m/s. If it takes 3 seconds for a sound wave to travel from the bottom of the ocean back to a ship, what is the depth of the water?

Check Your Progress

CHAPTER PROJECT 2

Test your musical instrument. Is it pleasing to the ear? Can you play a wide range of notes? Can you vary the loudness? Make further adjustments to your instrument. From what you have learned about pitch and frequency, what changes can you make to produce different notes? You may want to try tuning your instrument with a piano or pitch pipe. Try to play a musical scale or a simple song. Or make up your own song.

SECTION 1 The Nature of Sound

Key Ideas
◆ Sound is a disturbance that travels through a medium as a longitudinal wave.
◆ The speed of sound depends on the elasticity, density, and temperature of the medium.

Key Terms
larynx   elasticity   density

 SECTION 2 Properties of Sound

Key Ideas
◆ A sound wave of greater intensity sounds louder. Loudness is measured in decibels.
◆ The pitch of a sound that you hear depends on the frequency of the sound wave.
◆ As a sound source moves toward the listener, the waves reach the listener with a higher frequency. The pitch appears to increase because of the Doppler effect.

Key Terms
intensity   infrasound
loudness   pitch
decibels (dB)   Doppler effect
ultrasound

 SECTION 3 Combining Sound Waves

Key Ideas
◆ The blending of the fundamental tone and the overtones makes up the characteristic sound quality, or timbre, of a particular sound.
◆ Music is a set of tones that combine in ways that are pleasing to the ear.
◆ Noise has no pleasing timbre or identifiable pitch.
◆ Interference occurs when two or more sound waves interact.

Key Terms
timbre   noise   acoustics
music   dissonance   beats

 SECTION 4 How You Hear Sound

INTEGRATING LIFE SCIENCE

Key Ideas
◆ The outer ear funnels sound waves, the middle ear transmits the sound inward, and the inner ear converts the sound into a form your brain can understand.
◆ Many people suffer hearing loss as a result of injury, infection, or aging.

Key Terms
ear canal   middle ear
eardrum   cochlea

 SECTION 5 Applications of Sound

Key Ideas
◆ A sonar device measures the time it takes to detect reflected sound waves.
◆ Animals use sound waves to communicate, to navigate, and to find food.
◆ Doctors use ultrasound to "see" inside the human body and to diagnose and treat medical conditions.

Key Terms
sonar
echolocation
sonogram

USING THE INTERNET

www.science-explorer.phschool.com

CHAPTER 2 REVIEW

Reviewing Content

 For more review of key concepts, see the Interactive Student Tutorial CD-ROM.

Multiple Choice
Choose the letter of the best answer.

1. Sound does *not* travel through
   a. water.
   b. steel rails.
   c. wooden doors.
   d. outer space.
2. The Doppler effect causes an apparent change in
   a. loudness.
   b. intensity.
   c. pitch.
   d. resonance.
3. Beats result from
   a. reflection.
   b. refraction.
   c. diffraction.
   d. interference.
4. The hammer, anvil, and stirrup are in the
   a. outer ear.
   b. middle ear.
   c. inner ear.
   d. cochlea.
5. Sonar is used to find
   a. time.
   b. speed.
   c. angle of reflection.
   d. distance.

True or False
If the statement is true, write true. If it is false, change the underlined word or words to make the statement true.

6. Sound travels <u>faster</u> in air than in water.
7. Loudness is how the ear perceives <u>pitch</u>.
8. <u>Timbre</u> is what you hear as the quality of sound.
9. The <u>inner</u> ear contains the cochlea.
10. The system of using sound to measure distance is called <u>acoustics</u>.

Checking Concepts

11. When a drum vibrates, the air molecules that begin vibrating next to it do not reach your ear, yet you hear the sound of the drum. Explain.
12. As a car drives past you, the driver keeps a hand on the horn. Describe what you hear as the car approaches you then passes by.
13. What are the factors that affect the sound of a vibrating guitar string?
14. How can loud noises damage your hearing?
15. Why is ultrasound useful in medicine?
16. **Writing to Learn** You have been hired to produce an informational brochure about sound. This brochure will be presented to soon-to-arrive visitors from outer space. They have no concept of sound, and everything they learn will come from your brochure. Write a brief description of sound for the visitors.

Thinking Visually

17. **Concept Map** Copy the concept map about sound onto a separate sheet of paper. Then complete it and add a title. (For more on concept maps, see the Skills Handbook.)

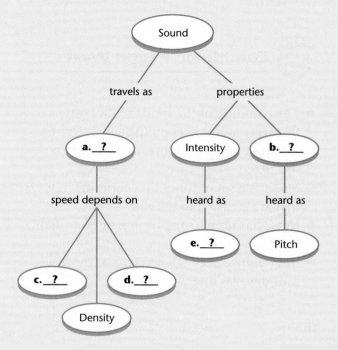

Applying Skills

The table below shows the range of frequencies produced and heard by various animals and birds. Use the data to answer Questions 18–20.

Animal	Highest Frequency Heard (Hz)	Highest Frequency Produced (Hz)
Human	20,000	1,100
Dog	50,000	1,800
Cat	65,000	1,500
Bat	120,000	120,000
Porpoise	150,000	120,000
Frog	10,000	8,000
Robin	21,000	13,000

18. Graphing Draw a bar graph to compare the highest frequencies heard by each animal and the highest frequencies produced by each animal.

19. Interpreting Data Which animal can hear the highest frequency?

20. Calculating If the speed of sound in air is 330 m/s, calculate the wavelength of the highest-frequency sound heard by humans. Use the following formula:

$$\text{Wavelength} = \frac{\text{Speed}}{\text{Frequency}}$$

Thinking Critically

21. Controlling Variables If you are measuring the speed of sound, what variable(s) should you try to keep constant?

22. Applying Concepts If one musician plays a note on an instrument and another plays a slightly higher note on a similar instrument, what will you hear?

23. Inferring Thunder and lightning happen at the same time. Why do you think you usually see the lightning before you hear the thunder?

24. Comparing and Contrasting How do sound waves behave like the waves in spring toys? How are they different?

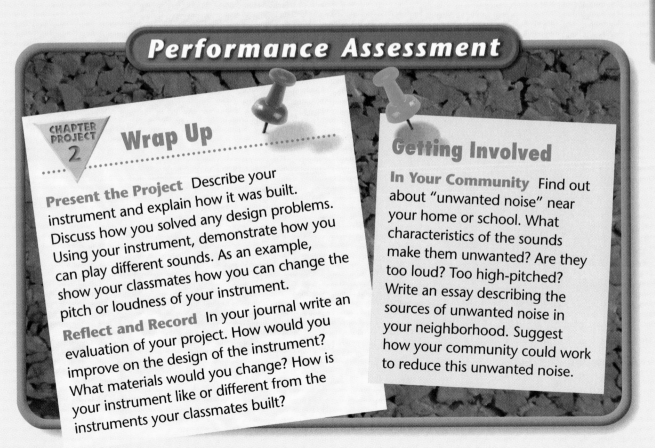

Performance Assessment

CHAPTER PROJECT 2 — Wrap Up

Present the Project Describe your instrument and explain how it was built. Discuss how you solved any design problems. Using your instrument, demonstrate how you can play different sounds. As an example, show your classmates how you can change the pitch or loudness of your instrument.

Reflect and Record In your journal write an evaluation of your project. How would you improve on the design of the instrument? What materials would you change? How is your instrument like or different from the instruments your classmates built?

Getting Involved

In Your Community Find out about "unwanted noise" near your home or school. What characteristics of the sounds make them unwanted? Are they too loud? Too high-pitched? Write an essay describing the sources of unwanted noise in your neighborhood. Suggest how your community could work to reduce this unwanted noise.

CHAPTER

3 The Electromagnetic Spectrum

These satellite dishes are used in long-distance communication.

WHAT'S AHEAD

SECTION

1 The Nature of Electro-magnetic Waves

Discover How Does a Beam of Light Travel?
Try This How Do Light Beams Behave?

SECTION

2 Waves of the Electro-magnetic Spectrum

Discover What Is White Light?
Try This What Does a Bee See?

SECTION

3 Producing Visible Light

Discover How Do Light Bulbs Differ?
Sharpen Your Skills Observing
Real-World Lab Comparing Light Bulbs

You're on the Air

Communication technology is developing at a rapid rate. Technology now makes it possible to store and process huge amounts of information. Communication technology will continue to improve as scientific advances are made. Look around you! How do people communicate? Radios, televisions, cellular phones, and electronic pagers are part of everyday life. Wireless communication has made it convenient for people to communicate anytime and anywhere.

In this chapter you will study and research the use of several wireless communication devices.

Your Goal To collect data about when, where, and why people use radios, televisions, cellular telephones, and other kinds of communication devices.

To complete this project you must
- design a survey sheet about the use of communication devices
- distribute your survey sheet to students in your school and to adults in your community
- compile and analyze your data
- create graphs to show your results

Get Started To get started, brainstorm what kinds of questions you will ask. Think about the format and content of your survey sheet. How might you involve students in other classes so you can gather more data?

Check Your Progress You will be working on this project as you study this chapter. To keep your project on track, look for Check Your Progress boxes at the following points.

Section 2 Review, page 88: Design and distribute your survey.
Section 4 Review, page 103: Compile, analyze, and graph your results.

Wrap Up At the end of the chapter (page 109), you will present the results of your survey to the class.

Integrating Technology 🌐

SECTION 4

Wireless Communication

Discover How Can Radio Waves Change?
Try This Produce Electromagnetic Interference
Real-World Lab Build a Crystal Radio

The Nature of Electromagnetic Waves

DISCOVER ·· ACTIVITY

How Does a Beam of Light Travel?

1. Punch a small hole (about 0.5 cm in diameter) in each of four large index cards.

2. Stand each card upright so that the long side of the index card is on the tabletop. Use binder clips or modeling clay to hold the cards upright.

3. Space the cards about 10 cm apart. To make sure the holes in the cards are in a straight line, run a piece of string through the four holes and pull it tight.

4. Place the flashlight in front of the card nearest you. Shut off all the lights, so that the only light you see comes from the flashlight. What do you see on the wall?

5. Move one of the cards sideways about 3 cm and repeat Step 4. Now what do you see on the wall?

Think It Over
Inferring Explain what happened in Step 5. What does this activity tell you about the path of light?

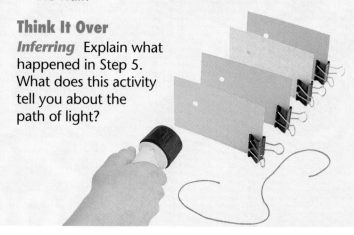

GUIDE FOR READING

◆ What is an electromagnetic wave?

◆ What is light?

Reading Tip As you read, keep a list of the words that are used to describe the nature of electromagnetic waves.

C lose your eyes for a moment and imagine you are in a shower of rain. Are you getting wet? Do you feel anything? Believe it or not, you are being "showered." Not by rain but by waves, most of which you cannot feel or hear. As you read this, you are surrounded by radio waves, infrared waves, visible light, ultraviolet waves, and maybe even tiny amounts of X-rays and gamma rays. If you have ever tuned a radio, spoken on a cordless or cellular phone, felt warmth on your skin, turned on a light, or had an X-ray taken, you have experienced electromagnetic waves.

Figure 1 Even though you cannot feel them, you are being showered by electromagnetic waves.

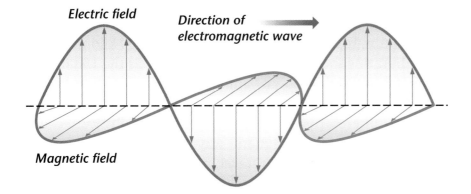

Electric field

Direction of electromagnetic wave

Magnetic field

Figure 2 An electromagnetic wave occurs when electric and magnetic fields vibrate at right angles to each other.

Electromagnetic Waves

You have seen waves travel through water and move along ropes and springs. You have also heard sound waves travel through air, metal, and water. All these waves have two things in common—they transfer energy from one place to another, and they require a medium through which to travel.

But a group of waves called electromagnetic waves can transfer energy without a medium. **Electromagnetic waves** are transverse waves that have some electrical properties and some magnetic properties. **An electromagnetic wave consists of changing electric and magnetic fields.**

Electric and Magnetic Fields Electromagnetic waves travel as vibrations in electric and magnetic fields. An electric field is a region in which charged particles can be pushed or pulled. Wherever there is an electric charge, there is an electric field associated with it. A moving electric charge is part of an electric current.

An electric current is surrounded by a magnetic field. A magnetic field is a region in which magnetic forces are present. If you place a paper clip near a magnet, the paper clip moves toward the magnet because of the magnetic field surrounding the magnet.

When the electric field changes, so does the magnetic field. The changing magnetic field causes the electric field to change. When one field vibrates, so does the other. In this way, the two fields constantly cause each other to change. The result is an electromagnetic wave, as shown in Figure 2.

Electromagnetic Radiation The energy that is transferred by electromagnetic waves is called **electromagnetic radiation.** Because electromagnetic radiation does not need a medium, it can travel through the vacuum of outer space. If it could not, light from the sun and stars could not travel through space to Earth. NASA officials could not make contact with space shuttles in orbit.

TRY THIS

How Do Light Beams Behave?

ACTIVITY

1. Fill two plastic cups with water. Slowly pour the water from the two cups into a sink. Aim the stream of water from one cup across the path of the water from the other cup.

2. How do the two streams interfere with each other?

3. Now darken a room and project a slide from a slide projector onto the wall. Shine a flashlight beam across the projector beam.

4. How do the two beams of light interfere with each other? What effect does the interference have on the projected picture?

Drawing Conclusions How is the interference between light beams different from that between water streams? Does this activity support a wave model or a particle model of light? Explain.

Speed of Electromagnetic Waves All electromagnetic waves travel at the same speed—about 300,000,000 meters per second in a vacuum. You can also think of this as 300,000 kilometers per second. At this speed, light from the sun travels the 150 million kilometers to Earth in about 8 minutes. Nothing can travel faster! When electromagnetic waves travel through a medium such as the atmosphere or glass, they travel more slowly. But even at slower speeds, electromagnetic waves travel about a million times faster than sound can travel in air.

✓ *Checkpoint* *What is the speed of electromagnetic waves in a vacuum?*

Waves or Particles?

In general, the wave model can explain many of the properties of electromagnetic radiation. However, some properties of electromagnetic radiation do not fit the wave model. **Light has many of the properties of waves. But light can also act as though it is a stream of particles.**

When light passes through a polarizing filter, it has the properties of a wave. An ordinary beam of light has waves that vibrate in all directions. A polarizing filter acts as though it has tiny slits that are either horizontal or vertical. When light enters a polarizing filter, only some waves can pass through. The light that passes through is called **polarized light.**

To help you understand polarization, think of waves of light as being like transverse waves on a rope. They vibrate up and down, left and right, or at any other angle. If you shake a rope through a fence with vertical slats, as shown in Figure 3, only waves that vibrate up and down will pass through. The other waves are blocked. A polarizing filter acts like the slats in a fence. It allows only waves that vibrate in one direction to pass through.

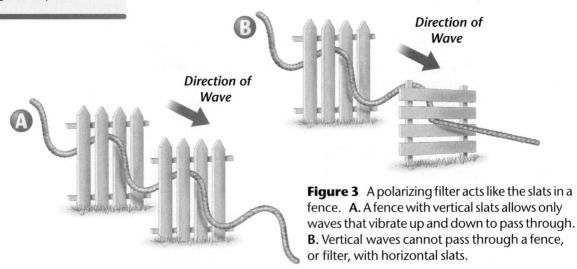

Figure 3 A polarizing filter acts like the slats in a fence. **A.** A fence with vertical slats allows only waves that vibrate up and down to pass through. **B.** Vertical waves cannot pass through a fence, or filter, with horizontal slats.

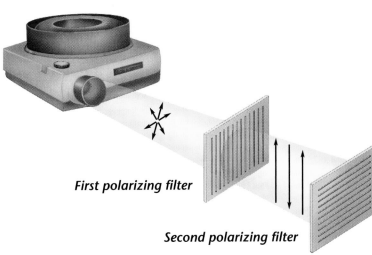

First polarizing filter

Second polarizing filter

Figure 4 The first polarizing filter allows only waves that vibrate up and down to pass through. When a second polarizing filter is placed in front of the first, and at right angles to it, no light passes through. *Applying Concepts Does the way that light passes through a polarizing filter support the wave model or the particle model of light?*

If you place one polarizing filter on top of another and rotate one of them, you will see how the amount of light coming through changes. If the two polarizing filters are placed so that one is rotated 90° from the other, no light can come through. All the light is blocked.

Here is an example of how light can act like a stream of particles. When a beam of light shines on some substances, it causes tiny particles called electrons to move. This movement causes an electric current to flow. Sometimes light can even knock electrons out of the substance. This is called the **photoelectric effect.** The photoelectric effect can only be explained by thinking of light as a stream of tiny packets, or particles, of energy. Each packet is called a **photon.** Albert Einstein first suggested that light travels as photons in 1905.

It may be difficult for you to picture light as being particles and waves at the same time. Many scientists find it difficult, too. But both models are necessary to explain all the properties of electromagnetic radiation.

Section 1 Review

1. What do electromagnetic waves consist of?
2. Describe one behavior that shows that light is a set of particles.
3. Describe one behavior that shows that light is a wave.
4. **Thinking Critically Comparing and Contrasting** How are light and sound alike? How are they different?

Science at Home

On the next sunny day, have family members go outside wearing their sunglasses. Compare the sunglasses. Which sunglasses have polarizing lenses? How can you tell? Through the sunglasses, look at surfaces that create glare, such as water or glass. Compare the effects of different pairs of sunglasses. Which kind of sunglasses are best designed to reduce glare on a sunny day? **CAUTION:** Do not look directly at the sun.

SECTION 2 Waves of the Electromagnetic Spectrum

DISCOVER •••••••••••••••••••••••••••••••••• ACTIVITY ••

What Is White Light?

1. Line the inside of a cardboard box with white paper. Hold a small triangular prism up to direct sunlight. **CAUTION:** *Do not look directly at the sun.*

2. Rotate the prism until the light coming out of the prism appears on the inside of the box. What colors do you see? What is the order of the colors? Describe how the colors progress from one to the next.

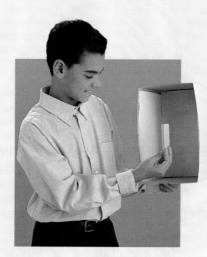

3. Using colored pencils, draw a picture of what you see inside the box.

Think It Over
Forming Operational Definitions The term *spectrum* describes a range. How do you think this term is related to what you just observed?

GUIDE FOR READING

◆ How do electromagnetic waves differ from each other?

◆ What are the waves of the electromagnetic spectrum?

Reading Tip Before you read, use the headings to make an outline about the different electromagnetic waves. As you read, make notes about each type of wave.

Can you imagine trying to keep food warm with a flashlight? How about trying to tune in a radio station on your television? Light and radio waves are both electromagnetic. But each has properties that make it useful for some purposes and useless for others. What makes radio waves different from light or ultraviolet rays?

Characteristics of Electromagnetic Waves

All electromagnetic waves travel at the same speed, but they have different wavelengths and different frequencies. Radiation in the wavelengths that your eyes can see is called visible light. Only a small portion of electromagnetic radiation is visible light. The rest of the wavelengths are invisible. Your radio detects wavelengths that are much longer and have a lower frequency than visible light.

Recall how speed, wavelength, and frequency are related:

$$\text{Speed} = \text{Wavelength} \times \text{Frequency}$$

Since the speed of all electromagnetic waves is the same, as the wavelength decreases, the frequency increases. Waves with the longest wavelengths have the lowest frequencies. Waves with the shortest wavelengths have the highest frequencies. The amount of energy carried by an electromagnetic wave increases with frequency. The higher the frequency of a wave, the higher its energy.

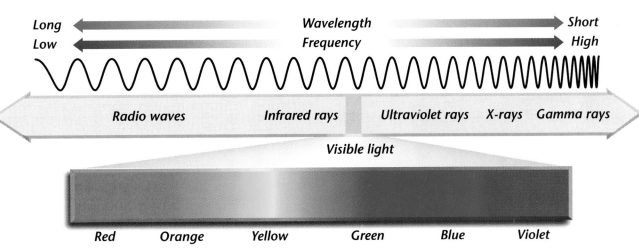

Figure 5 The electromagnetic spectrum shows the different electromagnetic waves in order of increasing frequency and decreasing wavelength.
Interpreting Diagrams Which electromagnetic waves have the highest frequencies?

The **electromagnetic spectrum** is the name for the range of electromagnetic waves when they are placed in order of increasing frequency. Figure 5 shows the electromagnetic spectrum. **The electromagnetic spectrum is made up of radio waves, infrared rays, visible light, ultraviolet rays, X-rays, and gamma rays.**

☑ *Checkpoint How are the frequency and wavelength of electromagnetic waves related?*

Radio Waves

Radio waves are the electromagnetic waves with the longest wavelengths and lowest frequencies. Like all electromagnetic waves, radio waves can travel through a vacuum. Most of the radio waves we receive, though, have traveled through air. Antennas pick up radio waves from the air and send them through wires to your radio. The radio converts the electromagnetic waves into the sound that comes out of the radio speakers.

Each radio station in an area broadcasts at a different frequency. To change the station on your radio, you adjust the tuning dial or press a button. This allows the tuner to pick up waves of a different frequency. The numbers on your radio tell you the frequency of the station you are listening to.

Microwaves The radio waves with the shortest wavelengths and the highest frequencies are **microwaves.** One of their most common uses is in microwave ovens. When you switch on a microwave oven, it gives off electromagnetic waves that bounce around inside the oven, penetrating the food. Water molecules in the food absorb the energy from the microwaves, causing the food to get hot.

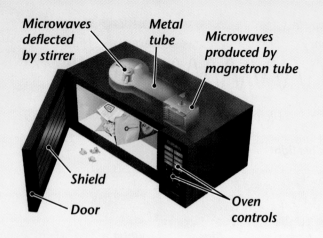

Microwaves deflected by stirrer

Metal tube

Microwaves produced by magnetron tube

Shield

Door

Oven controls

Figure 6 Microwaves produced in a microwave oven are absorbed by water molecules in foods. The energy raises the temperature of the food faster than an ordinary oven, so the food takes less time to cook. *Applying Concepts Why are metal containers not suitable for use in a microwave oven?*

Microwaves can pass right through some substances, such as glass and plastic. For this reason, microwaves do not heat glass and plastic containers. If the container gets hot, it is because the food in the container transfers heat to the container. Other substances, such as metals, reflect microwaves. If you have ever accidentally put a metal object, such as a spoon, into a microwave oven, you may have seen sparks. The sparks are the result of a buildup of electrical energy in the metal caused by the microwaves. Metal containers and utensils should never be used in microwave ovens.

Microwaves are not easily blocked by structures such as trees, buildings, and mountains. For this reason, microwaves are used to transmit cellular telephone calls. You will read more about cellular phones in Section 4.

Radar Short-wavelength microwaves are used in radar. **Radar,** which stands for **ra**dio **d**etection **a**nd **r**anging, can be used to locate objects. A radar device sends out short pulses of radio waves. Objects within a certain range reflect these waves. A receiver detects the reflected waves and measures the time it takes for them to come back. From the time and the known speed of the waves, the receiver calculates the distance to the object. Radar is used to monitor airplanes landing and taking off at airports, as Figure 7 shows. Radar is also used to locate ships at sea and to track weather systems.

In Chapter 2, you learned how the frequency of a sound wave seems to change when the source of the sound moves toward you or away from you. The Doppler effect occurs with electromagnetic waves too, and has some very useful applications. Police use radio waves and the Doppler effect to find the speeds of vehicles.

Figure 7 Radar is used to monitor airplanes taking off and landing at airports.

Figure 8 Radio waves and the Doppler effect are used to find the speeds of moving vehicles (left) and of moving balls at sporting events such as tennis matches (right).

A radar gun sends radio waves toward a moving car. The waves are then reflected. Because the car is moving, the frequency of the reflected waves is different from the frequency of the waves that are sent out. The radar device uses the difference in frequency to calculate the speed of the car. If the car is going faster than the speed limit, the police often give a speeding ticket.

Radar is also used at some sports events to measure the speed of a moving ball. The radio waves bounce off a moving ball. The speed at which the ball is hit or thrown can then be displayed on a board like the one in Figure 8.

Magnetic Resonance Imaging (MRI) Radio waves are also

INTEGRATING HEALTH used in medicine to produce pictures of tissues in the human body. This process is called **magnetic resonance imaging,** or MRI. In MRI, a person is placed in a machine that gives out short bursts of radio waves. The radio waves, combined with strong magnetic fields, cause atoms within the body to line up in the same direction. The atoms return to their original directions at different rates. By analyzing the responses, the MRI machine can create pictures of internal organs, including the brain. The pictures show clear images of muscles and other soft tissues that do not show up on X-rays. MRI is particularly useful in detecting brain and spine disorders.

✓ *Checkpoint* *What are three uses of radio waves?*

Infrared Rays

If you switch on an electric stove, you can feel infrared rays even before the element turns red. As the element gets warmer, it gives out energy that you feel as heat. This energy is infrared radiation, or infrared rays. **Infrared rays** have shorter wavelengths and higher

Figure 9 Magnetic resonance imaging (MRI) uses radio waves to create pictures of human tissue. It is used to examine the brain, spinal cord, and other organs.

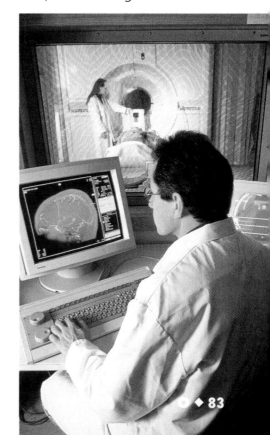

frequencies than radio waves. *Infra-* is a Latin prefix that means "below." So *infrared* means "below red." The next waves in the spectrum are red light.

Infrared rays range in wavelength from a little shorter than radio waves to just longer than visible light. Because you can feel the longest infrared rays as warmth, these rays are often called heat rays. Heat lamps have bulbs that give off more infrared rays and less visible light waves than regular bulbs. Some people have heat lamps in their bathrooms. You may also have seen heat lamps keeping food warm at cafeteria counters.

Most objects give off some infrared rays. Warmer objects give off infrared waves with more energy and higher frequencies than cooler objects. An infrared camera takes pictures using infrared

EXPLORING *the Electromagnetic Spectrum*

Electromagnetic waves are all around you——in your home, around your neighborhood and town, at the beach or pool, and in hospitals.

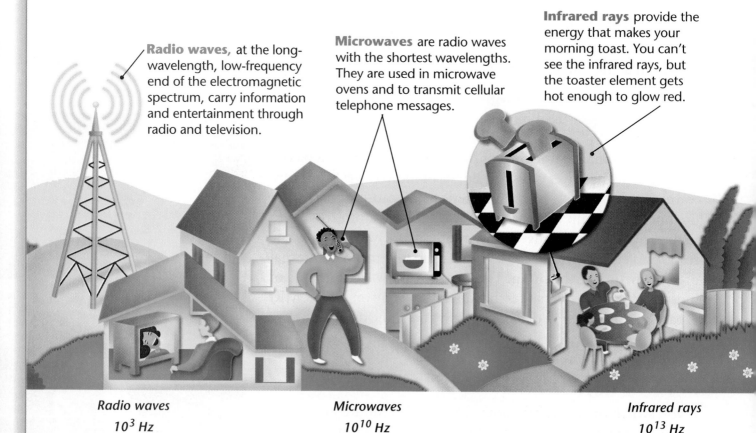

Radio waves, at the long-wavelength, low-frequency end of the electromagnetic spectrum, carry information and entertainment through radio and television.

Microwaves are radio waves with the shortest wavelengths. They are used in microwave ovens and to transmit cellular telephone messages.

Infrared rays provide the energy that makes your morning toast. You can't see the infrared rays, but the toaster element gets hot enough to glow red.

Radio waves	*Microwaves*	*Infrared rays*
10^3 Hz	*10^{10} Hz*	*10^{13} Hz*

rays instead of light. These pictures are called thermograms. A **thermogram** shows regions of different temperatures in different colors. Figure 10 shows a thermogram of a person. Thermograms identify the warm and cool parts of an object by analyzing infrared rays. Thermograms are especially useful for checking structures, such as houses, for energy leaks.

Even though your eyes cannot see the wavelengths of infrared rays, you can use an infrared camera or binoculars to detect people or animals in the dark. Satellites in space use infrared cameras to study the growth of plants and to observe the motions of clouds to help determine weather patterns.

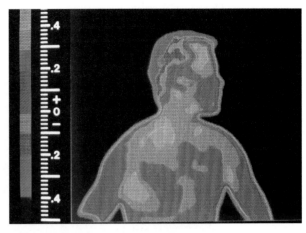

Figure 10 Infrared rays can be used to produce a thermogram. On a thermogram, regions of different temperatures appear in different colors.

Ultraviolet rays have wavelengths that are too short to see. In small quantities, they help your body produce vitamin D. In larger quantities, they can cause sunburn or even skin cancer.

X-rays can penetrate the body, but are absorbed by denser tissues, such as bone. These show up as the white parts on an X-ray image. X-rays that are not absorbed pass right through and cause the photographic film to darken when developed.

Gamma rays are used in hospitals to diagnose and treat cancer. They penetrate the body and concentrate in the tumor, killing it. Uncontrolled doses of gamma rays can cause cancer.

Visible light is the part of the spectrum you can see. Each different wavelength of light has a different color.

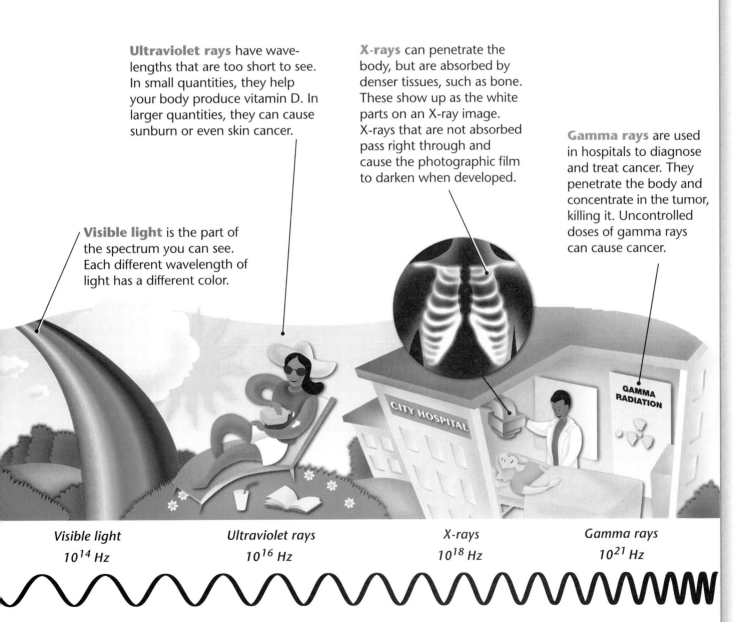

Visible light
10^{14} Hz

Ultraviolet rays
10^{16} Hz

X-rays
10^{18} Hz

Gamma rays
10^{21} Hz

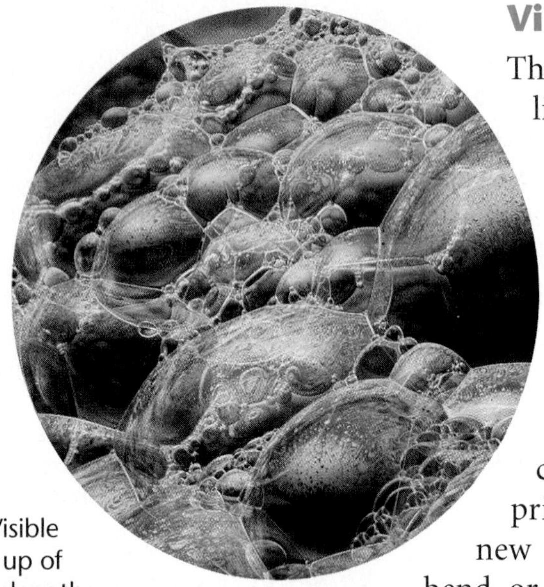

Visible Light

The electromagnetic waves that you can see are light. They make up only a small part of the electromagnetic spectrum. **Visible light** has shorter wavelengths and higher frequencies than infrared waves. The longest wavelengths of visible light are red. As the wavelengths decrease and the frequencies increase, you can see other colors of light. The shortest wavelengths are purple, or violet.

Have you ever seen a rainbow in the sky, colors on a bubble, or light passing through a prism? Recall what happens when waves enter a new medium, such as water or glass. The waves bend, or refract. Different wavelengths of light refract by different amounts, so the waves separate into the various colors. The colors in the visible spectrum are red, orange, yellow, green, blue, and violet, in order of increasing frequencies. Most visible light is made up of a mixture of these colors.

Checkpoint *What are the colors of the visible spectrum?*

Figure 11 Visible light is made up of different wavelengths. Each wavelength has its own color. When light passes through a bubble, interference produces the colors of the visible spectrum.

Ultraviolet Rays

Electromagnetic waves with wavelengths just shorter than those of visible light are called **ultraviolet rays,** or UV. *Ultra-* is a Latin prefix that means "beyond." So *ultraviolet* means "beyond violet." UV waves have higher frequencies than visible light, so they carry more energy. Because the energy of ultraviolet rays is great enough to damage or kill living cells, ultraviolet lamps are often used to kill bacteria on hospital equipment and in food processing plants.

Small doses of ultraviolet rays are beneficial to humans. Ultraviolet rays cause skin cells to produce vitamin D, which is needed for healthy bones and teeth. Ultraviolet lamps are used to treat jaundice, a condition of the liver that causes yellowing of the skin, in newborn babies.

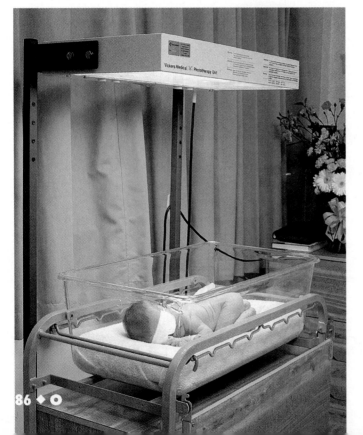

Figure 12 Ultraviolet light is used to treat jaundice in newborn babies. The baby's eyes are protected because too much ultraviolet light could damage them.

The ultraviolet rays present in sunlight can burn your skin. Too much exposure can cause skin cancer and damage your eyes. If you apply sunblock lotion and wear sunglasses, you can limit the damage to your body caused by UV rays.

INTEGRATING LIFE SCIENCE Although ultraviolet light is invisible to humans, many insects can see it. For example, bees have good color vision, but they do not see the same range of wavelengths that humans do. Bees see less of the lower frequency red waves and more of the higher frequency ultraviolet waves. Flowers that appear to be one color to a human appear very different to a honeybee. To the bee, the part of a flower that contains nectar looks different from the rest of the flower. The bee can head straight for the nectar!

X-Rays

X-rays are electromagnetic waves with very short wavelengths. Their frequencies are just a little higher than ultraviolet rays. Because of their high frequencies, X-rays carry more energy than ultraviolet rays and can penetrate most matter. Dense matter, such as bone or lead, absorbs X-rays and does not allow them to pass through. For this reason, X-rays are used to make images of bones inside the body. X-rays pass right through skin and soft tissues and cause the photographic film in the X-ray machine to darken when it is developed. The bones, which absorb X-rays, appear as the lighter areas on the film, as shown in Figure 13.

Too much exposure to X-rays can cause cancer. If you've ever had a dental X-ray, you'll remember how the dentist gave you a lead apron to wear during the procedure. The lead absorbs X-rays and prevents them from entering the body.

X-rays are sometimes used in industry and engineering. For example, to find out if a steel or concrete structure has tiny cracks, engineers can take an X-ray image of the structure. X-rays will pass through tiny cracks that are invisible to the human eye. Dark areas on the X-ray film show the cracks. This technology is often used to check the quality of joints in oil and gas pipelines.

What Does a Bee See?

Load a roll of UV-sensitive **ACTIVITY** film into a camera. Take photos of a variety of flowers. Include white flowers and flowers that you see bees near. Have the film developed and look at the prints.

Observing What can bees see that you cannot? How is this useful to the bees?

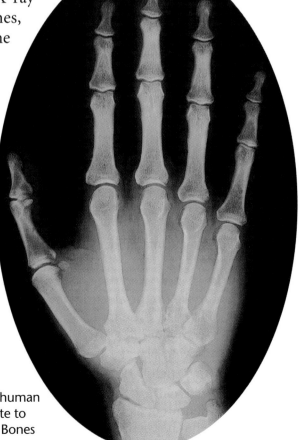

Figure 13 X-rays pass through softer human tissues and cause the photographic plate to darken behind them when developed. Bones absorb X-rays so they show up as lighter areas.

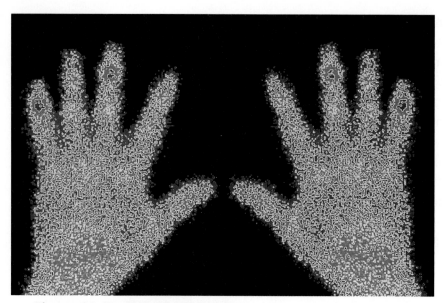

Figure 14 Doctors can inject radioactive liquids into the body and use gamma ray detectors to trace them. The detectors build images that doctors can use to examine the inside of the body.

Gamma Rays

Gamma rays have the shortest wavelengths and highest frequencies of the electromagnetic spectrum. Because they have the greatest amount of energy, they are the most penetrating of all the electromagnetic waves.

Some radioactive substances and certain nuclear reactions produce gamma rays. Because of their great penetrating ability, gamma rays can cause serious illness. However, when used in controlled conditions, gamma rays have some medical uses. For example, gamma rays can be used to kill cancer cells in radiation therapy. Gamma rays can also be used to examine the body's internal structures. A patient can be injected with a fluid that emits gamma rays. Then a gamma ray detector can form an image of the inside of the body.

 INTEGRATING SPACE SCIENCE Some objects far out in space give off bursts of gamma rays. The gamma rays travel for billions of years before they reach Earth. Earth's atmosphere blocks these gamma rays, so gamma-ray telescopes that detect them must orbit above Earth's atmosphere. Astronomers think that collisions of dying stars in distant galaxies could produce these gamma rays. Some gamma-ray telescopes also detect the stronger gamma rays given off in the atmosphere as a result of nuclear weapons tests on Earth.

Section 2 Review

1. How are all electromagnetic waves alike? How are they different?
2. List in order of increasing frequency the kinds of waves that make up the electromagnetic spectrum. Name one use for each.
3. Explain how radio waves are used to find the speed of a moving object.
4. How are X-rays useful? How are they dangerous?
5. **Thinking Critically Applying Concepts**
   As the wavelength of electromagnetic waves decreases, what happens to the frequency? To the energy?

Check Your Progress
Write the questions for your survey. Some categories you might want to include are types of communication devices, how often they are used, when and where they are used, and the purposes for which they are used. Do people use these devices for personal reasons or for business? (*Hint:* To make your survey easy to complete, ask questions that require short answers.) Give the survey sheet to your classmates and other students in the school for their families and neighbors to complete.

CHAPTER PROJECT 3

SCIENCE AND SOCIETY

Food Irradiation

Food sometimes travels a long way to reach your plate. Potatoes from Maine and strawberries from Florida or Mexico must stay fresh until you eat them. But every so often, food makes people ill. Millions of Americans get sick every year from contaminated or spoiled food.

One way to prevent such illness is food irradiation. In the most common method, gamma rays are sent through fresh or frozen food. The radiation slows decay and kills organisms that could make people sick. It makes food safer to eat and also helps the food stay fresh longer. Five minutes of irradiation will allow strawberries to stay fresh for an extra nine or ten days.

Some people worry about the possible dangers of eating irradiated food. More than 40 countries, including the United States, permit food irradiation. Others forbid it. Is food irradiation safe?

TREATED BY IRRADIATION

The Issues

Does Irradiation Destroy Nutrients in Food? Radiation kills living cells. But it can also make chemical changes in the food itself. It may destroy useful nutrients, such as vitamins A, B-1, E, and K. Up to ten percent of these vitamins can be lost when food is irradiated. Of course, other methods of protecting and preserving food—such as refrigeration or canning fruits and vegetables—also lead to small losses in nutrition. Even cooking food makes it lose some vitamins.

Does Irradiation Change the Food Itself? Irradiating food doesn't make the food radioactive. But irradiation may change the molecular structure of some foods, creating chemicals such as benzene and formaldehyde. In small doses, these substances have little effect. But large amounts can be harmful to people. Supporters say that these same substances are found naturally in food. Some critics say irradiation should not be used until

there is further research. Researchers want to determine whether people who eat irradiated food for a long time are more likely to develop cancer or other diseases. Other experts say that the short-term research already done shows that irradiation is safe. Some alternatives to irradiation, such as spraying with pesticides, are clearly more harmful.

Will Irradiating Food Make People Less Careful About Handling Food? In the United States, all irradiated food must be labeled. But if people are not careful about washing their hands before preparing food, irradiated food can still become contaminated. Also, the amounts of radiation allowed won't kill all harmful organisms. It's still necessary to cook food properly before eating it, especially meat and eggs. Some food experts worry that irradiation will make people feel falsely safe and become careless about preparing food.

You Decide

1. Identify the Problem

In your own words, explain the problem of food irradiation.

2. Analyze the Options

List reasons for and against: (a) requiring all food to be irradiated; (b) permitting, but not requiring, food irradiation; and (c) banning food irradiation.

3. Find a Solution

You see two containers of a food at the supermarket. One is irradiated; one is not. The price is the same. Which would you buy? Explain why.

SECTION 3 Producing Visible Light

DISCOVER

How Do Light Bulbs Differ?

1. Your teacher will give you one incandescent and one fluorescent light bulb.

2. Examine each bulb closely. What is the shape and size of each? Describe the differences between the bulbs. Draw each type of bulb and record your observations.

3. How do you think each bulb produces light?

Think It Over
Posing Questions Make a list of five questions you could ask to help you understand how each bulb works.

GUIDE FOR READING

◆ What are the different types of light bulbs?

◆ What colors of light are produced by an incandescent bulb?

Reading Tip As you read, compare and contrast the different ways in which light can be produced.

Figure 15 An incandescent light bulb glows when electricity passes through the tungsten filament. *Inferring Why do incandescent bulbs get so hot?*

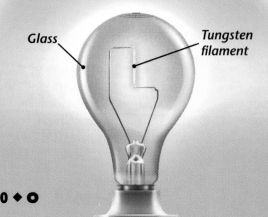

Glass

Tungsten filament

Look around the room. Most of the objects you see are visible because they reflect light. If no light source were present, you could not see the objects. An object that can be seen because it reflects light is an **illuminated** object. Light illuminates the page you are reading and your desk. An object that gives off its own light is a **luminous** object. A light bulb, a burning match, and the sun are examples of luminous objects.

There are many different types of lighting. **Common types of lighting include incandescent, fluorescent, neon, sodium vapor, and tungsten-halogen light bulbs.** Some light bulbs produce a continuous spectrum of wavelengths. Others produce only a few wavelengths of light. You can use an instrument called a **spectroscope** to view the different colors of light produced by each type of bulb.

Incandescent Lights

Have you heard the phrase "red hot"? When some objects get hot enough, they glow, giving off a faint red light. If they get even hotter, the glow turns into white light. The objects are said to be "white hot." **Incandescent lights** (in kun DES unt) glow when a filament inside them gets hot.

Look closely at a clear, unlit incandescent bulb. You'll notice that inside is a thin wire coil called a filament. It is made of a metal called tungsten. When an electric current passes through this filament, it heats up. When the filament gets hot enough, it gives off red light, which has low frequencies. As it gets hotter, the filament begins to give off light waves with higher

90 ◆ O

frequencies. Once the filament gets hot enough to give off violet light, all the frequencies of light combine, producing white light. **Incandescent lights give off all the colors of visible light: red, orange, yellow, green, blue, and violet.**

The American inventor Thomas Edison is credited with developing a long-lasting incandescent light bulb in 1879. Edison knew that if he passed an electric current through a wire, it would get hot and glow. By experimenting with different types of filaments, Edison developed a light bulb that would glow for a long time.

Incandescent bulbs are not very efficient in giving off light. Less than ten percent of the energy is actually given out as light. Most of the energy produced by an incandescent bulb is given off as infrared rays. This is why incandescent bulbs can get quite hot when they have been left on for a while.

Fluorescent Lights

Have you ever noticed the long, narrow light bulbs in stores and offices? They are **fluorescent lights** (floo RES uhnt). Maybe you have some in your school. Each glass tube contains a gas and is coated on the inside with a powder.

When an electric current passes through a fluorescent bulb, it causes the gas to emit ultraviolet waves. When the ultraviolet waves hit the powder coating inside the tube, the coating emits visible light. This process is called fluorescing.

Unlike incandescent lights, fluorescent lights give off most of their energy as light. They usually last longer than incandescent bulbs and use less electricity, which makes them less expensive to run.

☑ *Checkpoint* *Why are fluorescent bulbs more economical than incandescent bulbs?*

Sharpen your Skills

Observing ACTIVITY

Use a spectroscope to observe light from different sources. **CAUTION:** *Do not look at the sun with the spectroscope.*

1. Look through the spectroscope at an incandescent light. Using colored pencils, draw and label the band of colors as they appear in the spectroscope.

2. Now, look at a fluorescent light through the spectroscope. Again, draw and label what you see.

How are the two bands of color the same? How are they different? Can you explain the differences?

Figure 16 Fluorescent lights are commonly used in offices, stores, and schools. They are efficient and inexpensive.

Figure 17 Neon lights are used in advertising signs and decoration. *Applying Concepts Why are neon lights so colorful?*

Neon Lights

Some gases can be made to produce light by passing an electric current through them. For example, a **neon light** consists of a sealed glass tube filled with neon. When an electric current passes through the neon, particles of the gas absorb energy. However, the gas particles cannot hold the energy for very long. The energy is released in the form of light. This process is called electric discharge through gases.

Pure neon gives out red light. Often, what is called a neon light has a different gas, or a mixture of gases, in the tube. Different gases produce different colors of light. For example, both argon gas and mercury vapor produce greenish blue light. Helium gives a golden yellow light. Krypton gives a pale violet light. Sometimes the gases are put into colored glass tubes to produce other colors. Neon lights are commonly used for bright, flashy signs.

Sodium Vapor Lights

Sodium vapor lights contain a small amount of solid sodium as well as some neon and argon gas. When the neon and argon gas are heated, they begin to glow. This glow heats up the sodium, causing it to change from a solid into a gas. The particles of sodium vapor give off energy in the form of yellow light.

Sodium vapor lights are commonly used for street lighting. They require very little electricity to give off a great deal of light, so they are quite economical.

Figure 18 Sodium vapor light bulbs give off a yellow light. They are commonly used to illuminate streets and parking lots.

Tungsten-Halogen Lights

Tungsten-halogen lights work partly like incandescent bulbs. They have tungsten filaments and contain a gas. The gas is one of a group of gases called the halogens. When electricity passes through the filament, the filament gets hot and glows. The halogen makes the filament give off a bright white light.

Tungsten-halogen lights have become very popular because they provide bright light from small bulbs, but use very little electricity. They are used in overhead projectors and also in floor lamps. Because halogen bulbs become very hot, they must be kept away from flammable materials, such as paper and curtains.

Figure 19 Tungsten-halogen light bulbs contain a tungsten filament and a halogen gas. Even small bulbs can produce very bright light.

Bioluminescence

INTEGRATING LIFE SCIENCE Have you ever seen a firefly? On a warm summer evening, they flash their lights in patterns to attract mates. Fireflies are examples of organisms that produce their own light in a process called bioluminescence. **Bioluminescence** (by oh loo muh NES uns) occurs as a result of a chemical reaction among proteins and oxygen in an organism. The reaction produces energy that is given off in the form of light. Unlike a light bulb, which gives off most of its energy as infrared rays, the reaction that produces bioluminescence gives off almost all of its energy as light.

There are also bioluminescent organisms in the oceans. Some types of jellyfish give off light when they are disturbed. Deep in the ocean, where sunlight cannot reach, bioluminescence is the only source of light. Some deep-sea fish use bioluminescence to search for food or to attract mates.

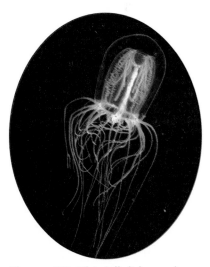

Figure 20 This jellyfish produces its own light by bioluminescence.

Section 3 Review

1. What are five common types of lighting?
2. How does an incandescent light bulb work?
3. Compare luminous objects with illuminated objects. Give two examples of each.
4. Why are fluorescent lights commonly used in businesses and schools?
5. **Thinking Critically Making Judgments** Make a list of the different rooms in your home. Which type of light do you think is best for each room? Give reasons for each choice.

Science at Home

Invite family members to visit a hardware store that sells light bulbs. Ask the salesperson to describe the different kinds of bulbs available. Read the information about each bulb on the side panel of each package. Ask the salesperson to explain any terms you don't understand. Look for the cost and expected life of the bulbs, too. How does this information help you and your family purchase the most economical bulbs?

You, the Consumer

Comparing Light Bulbs

In this lab, you will design an experiment to compare the illumination provided by different light bulbs.

Problem

Which light bulb provides the best illumination?

Skills Focus

designing experiments, controlling variables, measuring, drawing conclusions

Materials (per group)

a variety of incandescent light bulbs that can fit in the same lamp or socket
medium-sized cardboard box
light socket or lamp (without shade)
meter stick   wax paper
scissors   plain paper

Procedure

1. Following the instructions below, construct your own light box. The box allows you to test the illumination that is provided by each light bulb.
2. With a partner, examine the different bulbs. What is the power (watts), light output (lumens), and life (hours) for each bulb? Predict which light bulb will be the brightest. Explain your choice.
3. How will you test your prediction?
   ◆ What kinds of incandescent light bulbs will you use?
   ◆ What variables will you keep constant? What variables will you change?
4. Make a data table like the one shown at the right to record your data.
5. Review your plan. Will your procedure help you find an answer to the problem?

How to Build and Use a Light Box

A. Use a medium-sized cardboard box, such as the kind of box copy paper comes in. If the box has flaps, cut them off.

B. Carefully cut a viewing hole (about 2 cm × 4 cm) in the bottom of the box. This will be on top when the box is used. This is hole A.

C. Punch another hole (about 1 cm × 1 cm) on one side of the box. This is hole B. It will allow light from the bulb to enter the box.

D. To decrease the amount of light that can enter, cover hole B with two layers of wax paper.

E. Put one of your light bulbs in the lamp and place it to the side of the box, about 1 m from hole B.

F. Have your partner write a secret letter on a piece of plain paper. Put the paper on the table. Place the light box over the paper with the viewing hole facing up.

G. Now look through hole A.

H. Turn the lamp on and move the light toward the box until you can read the secret letter. Measure the distance between the light bulb and hole B.

DATA TABLE

Bulb #	Brand Name	Power (watts)	Light Output (lumens)	Life (hrs)	Cost ($)	Distance from Bulb to Light Box (cm)

6. Ask your teacher to check your procedure.

7. Before you repeat the steps for a second light bulb, look back at your procedure. How could you improve the accuracy of your results?

8. Test the illumination of the rest of your light bulbs.

Analyze and Conclude

1. How does the distance between the bulb and hole B affect how easily you can read the secret letter?

2. Based on your observations, what can you infer about the illumination provided by each bulb? Which bulb gave the most illumination?

3. How did your results compare with your prediction? What did you learn that you did not know when you made your prediction?

4. What factors affect the illumination given by a light bulb?

5. Apply Based on your results, do you think that the most expensive bulb is the best?

More to Explore

Modify your light box and repeat the activity. What different materials would you use? Would you make the light box smaller or larger than the original? How do different light boxes compare in testing illumination by light bulbs?

SECTION 4 Wireless Communication

DISCOVER ·····························ACTIVITY····

How Can Radio Waves Change?

1. Trace the wave diagram onto a piece of tracing paper. Then transfer the wave diagram onto a flat piece of latex from a balloon or latex glove.

2. Stretch the latex horizontally. How is the stretched wave different from the wave on the tracing paper?

3. Now stretch the latex vertically. How is this wave different from the wave on the tracing paper? How is it different from the wave in Step 2?

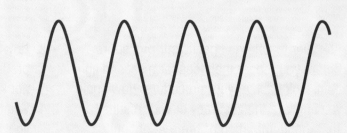

Think It Over

Making Models Which stretch changes the amplitude of the wave? Which stretch changes the frequency of the wave?

GUIDE FOR READING

◆ How are radio waves used to transmit information?

◆ How do cellular phones and pagers use electromagnetic waves?

◆ How are satellites used to relay information?

Reading Tip Before you read, preview the diagrams and captions in the section. List any terms you are not familiar with. As you read, write the definition of each term on your list.

Recent advances in technology have turned our world into a global village. Today it is possible to communicate with people on the other side of the world in just seconds. You can watch a television broadcast of a soccer game from Europe or a news report from the Middle East. Once scientists discovered that messages could be carried on electromagnetic waves, they realized that communication signals could travel at the speed of light.

Radio and Television

How does your favorite radio station or television program travel to you? Both radio and television programs are carried, or transmitted, by radio waves. Radio transmissions are produced when charged particles move back and forth in transmission antennas. These transmissions are broadcast, or sent out in all directions. Radio waves carry information from the antenna of a broadcasting station to the receiving antenna of your radio or television. Don't confuse the sound that comes from your radio with radio waves. Your radio converts the radio transmission into sound waves.

There are many different radio and television stations, all sending out signals. So how can each individual program or song come through clearly? As you move your radio tuner up and down the dial, you can hear different radio stations. Look at the radio dial in Figure 21. Each number on the dial represents a dif-

Figure 21 The radio dial shows the FM and AM frequency bands. Each radio station is assigned a different carrier frequency.

ferent frequency measured either in kilohertz (kHz) or megahertz (MHz).

Recall that a hertz is one cycle per second. If something vibrates 1,000 times a second, it has a frequency of 1,000 Hz, or 1 kilohertz (kHz). (The prefix *kilo-* means "one thousand.") If something vibrates 1,000,000 times a second, it has a frequency of 1,000,000 Hz, or 1 megahertz (MHz). (The prefix *mega-* means "one million.")

In the United States, the Federal Communications Commission, or FCC, assigns different frequencies of radio waves for different uses. Radio stations are allowed to use one part of the spectrum, and television stations use other parts. Taxi and police radios are also each assigned a set of frequencies. In this way, the entire spectrum of radio waves is divided into bands that are used for different purposes.

Each radio or television station is assigned a basic broadcast frequency, known as a carrier frequency. Each station is identified by the frequency at which it broadcasts. Radio stations broadcast in one of two main frequency bands—AM and FM.

AM Radio AM stands for **amplitude modulation.** On AM broadcasts, the frequency of the wave remains constant. The information that will become sound, such as speech and music, is coded in changes, or modulations, in the amplitude of the wave. **At the broadcasting station, music and speech are converted from sound into electronic signals. The electronic signals for AM broadcasts are then converted into a pattern of changes in the amplitude of a radio wave.**

Figure 22 Sound signals are carried by varying either the amplitude (AM) or the frequency (FM) of radio waves.
Interpreting Diagrams What remains constant in the AM wave? In the FM wave?

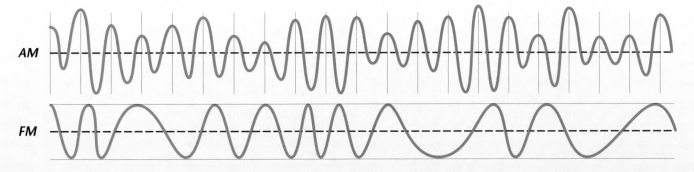

AM

FM

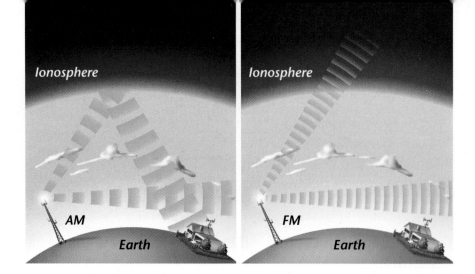

Figure 23 AM radio waves are reflected by the ionosphere. FM radio waves pass through the ionosphere. *Applying Concepts Which type of broadcast has a longer range on Earth?*

Your radio picks up the wave and converts the coded information back into an electronic signal. This signal travels to your radio's speaker and comes out as sound waves.

The AM frequencies used for radio broadcasts range from 535 kHz to 1,605 kHz. These radio waves vibrate at frequencies ranging from 535 to 1,605 thousand times per second.

AM waves have relatively long wavelengths and are easily reflected by Earth's ionosphere. The ionosphere is an electrically charged layer high in the atmosphere. Figure 23 shows how this reflection allows the AM waves to "bend" around the curvature of Earth's surface. This is why AM radio stations can broadcast over long distances, especially at night when the absorption of radio waves by the ionosphere is reduced. However, the reception of AM waves is sometimes not very clear. For this reason, AM radio stations usually broadcast more talk shows than music.

FM Radio FM stands for **frequency modulation.** On FM broadcasts, the amplitude of the wave remains constant. **FM signals travel as changes, or modulations, in the frequency of the wave.**

If you look at an FM dial on a radio, you will see that the stations broadcast at frequencies from 88 MHz to 108 MHz. FM radio waves vibrate from 88 million to 108 million times each second. The frequencies of FM stations are much higher than the frequencies of AM radio stations, which vibrate only thousands of times per second.

Because FM waves have higher frequencies and more energy than AM waves, they penetrate the atmosphere instead of being reflected back to Earth. For this reason, FM waves do not travel as far as AM waves. If you've ever gone on a long car trip with the radio on, you have probably lost reception of radio stations and had to tune in new ones as you traveled. FM waves are usually received clearly and produce a better sound quality than AM waves. They are generally used to broadcast music.

Produce Electromagnetic Interference

ACTIVITY

Find out which appliances produce radio waves.

1. Turn on a non-cabled television set. Keep the volume low. Observe the image on the screen.
2. Plug an electric mixer or a hair dryer into a nearby outlet and switch it on. What happens to the image on the television?
3. Change the speed of the mixer or hair dryer. What happens to the image on the television?

Drawing Conclusions What can you conclude about the electric mixer or the hair dryer? Explain.

Television Television broadcasts are similar to radio broadcasts, except that the electromagnetic waves carry picture signals as well as sound. There are two main bands of television wave frequencies: Very High Frequency (VHF) and Ultra High Frequency (UHF). VHF television channels range from frequencies of 54 MHz to 216 MHz, and correspond to Channels 2 through 13 on your television set. This band of frequencies includes some FM radio frequencies, so television stations are restricted from using the frequencies that are reserved for radio stations. UHF channels range from frequencies of 470 MHz to 806 MHz, and correspond to Channels 14 through 69.

Weather can affect the reception of television signals. For better reception, cable companies now pick up the signals, improve them, and send them through cables into homes. Cable television reception is usually clearer than reception with an antenna. About half of American homes that have television now have cable reception.

☑ *Checkpoint* *What do the terms VHF and UHF mean?*

Cellular Telephones

Cellular phones have become very common. **Cellular telephones transmit and receive signals using high-frequency radio waves, or microwaves.** The cellular system works over regions divided up into many small cells. Each cell has its own transmitter and receiver. Cells that are next to each other are assigned different frequencies, but cells that are not next to each other can be assigned the same frequency. Cellular telephone signals are strong enough to reach only a few nearby cells. They cannot travel great distances. This allows many phones in different areas to use the same frequency at the same time, without interfering with each other.

As cellular phone users travel from one cell to another, the signals are transferred from one cell to another with very little interruption. If you travel outside one cellular phone company's area, another company becomes responsible for transmitting the signals.

Most cellular phones are more expensive to use than wired phones. But they are becoming more and more affordable. Cellular phones allow users to make and receive calls without having to use someone else's phone or look for a pay phone.

Figure 24 Cellular telephones transmit and receive radio waves that travel short distances.

Cordless Telephones

Cellular telephones should not be confused with cordless telephones. Cordless telephones are connected to the telephone system just like ordinary phones. The only difference is that there is no cord between the handset and the base. The information is transmitted from the handset to the base by radio waves, so you can walk away from the base as you talk on the phone.

Pagers

Pagers are small electronic devices that people can carry in their pockets or attach to their clothes. To page someone, you must

Wireless Communication

Since the late 1800s, many developments in communication have turned our world into a global village.

1895
First Wireless Transmission

Italian engineer and inventor Guglielmo Marconi successfully used radio waves to send a coded wireless signal a distance of more than 2 km.

1923
Ship-to-Ship Communication

For the first time, people on one ship could talk to people on another. The signals were sent as electromagnetic waves, received by an antenna, and converted into sound.

1900

1920

1888
Electromagnetic Waves

German scientist Heinrich Hertz proved James Clerk Maxwell's prediction that radio waves exist. Hertz demonstrated that the waves could be reflected, refracted, diffracted, and polarized just like light waves.

1901
First Transatlantic Signals

On December 12, the first transatlantic radio signal was sent from Poldhu Cove, Cornwall, England, to Signal Hill, Newfoundland. The coded electromagnetic waves traveled more than 3,000 km through the air.

Cornwall, England

Signal Hill, Newfoundland

dial the telephone number of the pager. This can be done from a telephone or another pager. Depending on the pager, you can then enter your telephone number or leave a voice message. Some pagers even allow the user to receive text messages.

When you leave a message for a pager, the information is first sent to a receiving station. There it is coded and sent as electromagnetic waves to the correct pager. The pager then beeps or vibrates, letting the owner know that there is a message. Some pagers are two-way pagers. This means that the pager can return electromagnetic signals to the receiving station, which sends them to the person who sent the original message.

In Your Journal

At your local or school library, find out more about Guglielmo Marconi. Imagine you were hired as his assistant. Write a letter to a friend that describes your new job.

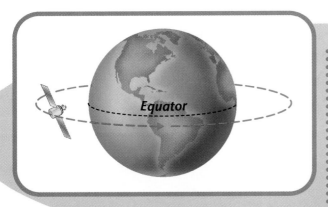

Equator

1963
Geosynchronous Orbit

Communications satellites are launched into orbits at altitudes of about 35,000 km. At this altitude, a satellite orbits Earth at the same rate as Earth rotates. A satellite orbiting above the equator remains above the same location as Earth turns.

1940   **1960**   **1980**

1957
Sputnik I

On October 4, the Soviet Union became the first country to successfully launch an artificial satellite into orbit. This development led to a new era in communications. Since then, more than 5,000 artificial satellites have been placed in orbit.

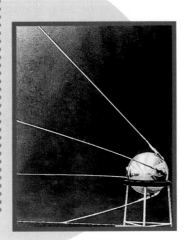

1979
Cellular Phone Network

The world's first cellular phone network was set up in Japan. It allowed people to make and receive telephone calls without wired phones.

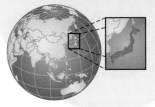

Communications Satellites

Since the development of satellite technology, long-distance communications have become faster and cheaper. Communications satellites work like the receivers and transmitters of a cellular phone system. Satellites orbiting Earth receive radio, television, and telephone signals, and transmit them around the world. **The radio waves are sent from Earth up to the satellite, which then relays the waves to other receivers on Earth.** Most satellites strengthen the signals before sending them back to Earth. Communications satellites can relay several signals at the same time.

Because a satellite can only "see" part of Earth at any given time, it is necessary to have more than one satellite in orbit for any given purpose. In this way, signals can be sent all around the world at any time.

Satellite Telephone Systems In recent years, the use of telephones has increased so much that telephone companies have had to develop new ways of transmitting electromagnetic waves. Several companies have developed satellite telephone systems. The radio waves are sent up through the atmosphere, received by one of the communications satellites, and transmitted back to Earth. This system makes long-distance telephone calls more easily available and less costly.

Figure 25 Communications satellites are remote-controlled spacecraft that orbit Earth. Because electromagnetic waves travel in straight lines, they cannot curve around Earth. Satellites receive signals from Earth and transmit them to parts of the world they could not otherwise reach.

Television Satellites Television networks use communications satellites to send their signals to local stations across the country. The television signals are changed into radio waves using frequency modulation.

Some people have their own antennas to receive signals directly from satellites. Because the antennas are dish-shaped, they are known as satellite dishes. Older satellite dishes were very large, but as frequencies of broadcast signals have changed, the dishes have become a lot smaller. Also, modern satellites are much more powerful.

The Global Positioning System The Global Positioning System (GPS) was originally designed for use by the United States military. Now, many thousands of civilians use the system for navigation. The Global Positioning System uses a group of two dozen communications satellites that work together. The GPS satellites broadcast radio signals to Earth. These signals carry information that can tell you your exact location on Earth's surface, or even in the air. Anybody on Earth with a GPS receiver can receive these signals.

Today, GPS receivers are becoming increasingly common in airplanes, boats, and even in cars. In some cars you can type your destination into a computer and have the GPS system map out your route. A computerized voice might even tell you when to turn right or left.

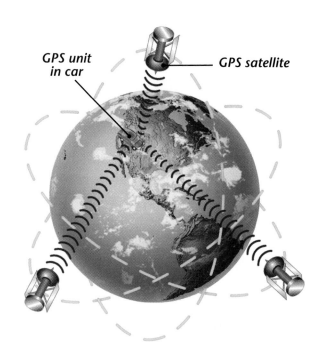

Figure 26 The Global Positioning System (GPS) uses a group of 24 satellites, each traveling in its own orbit. Receivers in cars, boats, and airplanes use signals from at least three satellites to determine their exact location on Earth.

Section 4 Review

1. Describe how the sounds in a radio station such as speech or music are converted into radio waves.
2. What is the difference between AM and FM radio broadcasts?
3. How does the cellular phone system work?
4. How does a satellite relay radio and television signals?
5. **Thinking Critically** **Predicting** What do you think might happen if the Federal Communications Commission did not control the use of different frequencies of radio waves?

Check Your Progress

CHAPTER PROJECT 3

Collect your surveys and tally your results. As you analyze your data, look for patterns. You can use bar graphs or circle graphs to display your findings. Include information about cost, time, and any other questions you asked in your survey. Write one or two paragraphs explaining your conclusions.

Build a Crystal Radio

The first radio, called a crystal set, was invented in the early 1900s. At first, people built their own crystal sets to receive broadcast transmissions from local radio stations. In this lab, you will build your own crystal radio and learn how it works.

Problem

How can you build a device that can collect and convert radio signals?

Skill Focus

measuring, observing, problem solving, drawing conclusions

Materials (per group)

cardboard tube (paper towel roll)
3 pieces of enameled or insulated wire, 1 about 30 m long, and 2 about 30 cm long
wirestrippers or sandpaper
2 alligator clips
scissors
aluminum foil
2 pieces of cardboard (sizes can range from 12.5 cm × 20 cm to 30 cm × 48 cm)
masking tape
crystal diode
earphone
2 pieces of insulated copper antenna wire, 1 about 30 m long, and 1 about 0.5m long

Procedure

Part 1 Wind the Radio Coil

(*Hint:* All ends of the insulated wires need to be stripped to bare metal. If the wire is enameled, you need to sandpaper the ends.)

1. Carefully punch two holes approximately 2.5 cm apart in each end of a cardboard tube. The holes should be just large enough to thread the insulated wire through.
2. Feed one end of the 30-m piece of insulated wire through one set of holes. Leave a 50-cm lead at that end. Attach alligator clip #1 to this lead. See Figure 1.
3. Wind the wire tightly around the cardboard tube. Make sure the coils are close together but do not overlap one another.
4. Wrap the wire until you come to the end of the tube. Feed the end of the wire through the other set of holes, leaving a 50-cm lead as before. Attach alligator clip #2 to this lead. See Figure 2.

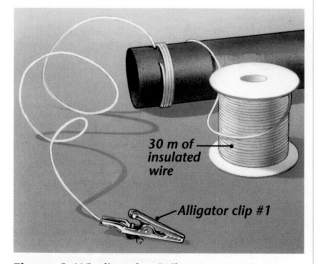

30 m of insulated wire

Alligator clip #1

Figure 1 Winding the Coil

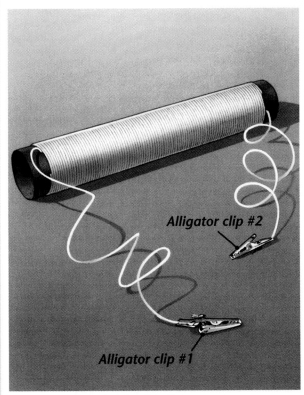

Figure 2 The Finished Coil

Part 2 Make the Tuning Plates

5. Without wrinkling the aluminum foil, cover one side of each piece of cardboard with the foil. Trim off any excess foil and tape the foil in place.

6. Hold the pieces of cardboard together with the foil facing inward. Tape along one edge to make a hinge. It is important for the foil pieces to be close together but not touching. See Figure 3.

7. Make a small hole through the cardboard and foil near a corner of one side. Feed one of the short pieces of insulated wire through the hole and tape it onto the foil as shown. Tape the other short piece of insulated wire to the corner of the other side. See Figure 4.

8. Connect one end of the wire from the foil to alligator clip #1. Connect the other wire from the foil to alligator clip #2.

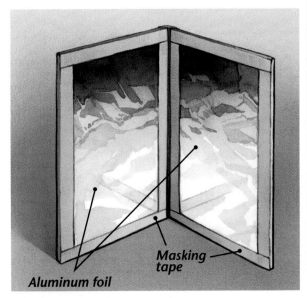

Figure 3 The Tuning Plates

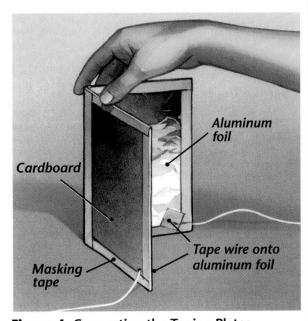

Figure 4 Connecting the Tuning Plates

Part 3 Prepare the Earphone

9. Handle the diode carefully. Connect one wire from the diode to alligator clip #1. The arrow on the diode should point to the earphone. Tape the other end of the diode wire to one of the earphone wires.

10. Connect the other wire from the earphone to alligator clip #2. See Figure 5.

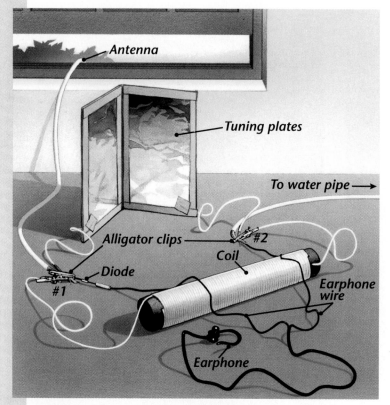

Figure 5 The Completed Radio

Part 4 Hook Up the Antenna

11. String the long piece of antenna wire along the floor to an outside window. Connect the other end of the wire to alligator clip #1.

12. Connect one end of the shorter piece of antenna wire to a cold-water pipe or faucet. Connect the other end to alligator clip #2. See Figure 5.

13. Put on the earphone and try to locate a station by squeezing the tuning plates slowly until you hear a signal. Some stations will come in when the plates are close together. Other stations will come in when the plates are opened far apart.

Analyze and Conclude

1. How many stations can you pick up? Where are the stations located geographically? Which station has the strongest signal? Keep a log of the different stations you receive.

2. How does adjusting the tuning plates affect the radio signals?

3. A crystal radio is not a powerful receiver. You can improve reception by having a good antenna. How can you improve your antenna?

4. **Apply** What are the similarities and differences between a modern radio and a crystal radio? How is one more efficient?

Design an Experiment

Use your crystal radio or any radio to test signal reception at various times of the day. Do you receive more stations at night or in the morning? Why do you think certain times of the day are better for receiving radio waves?

STUDY GUIDE

SECTION 1 — The Nature of Electromagnetic Waves

Key Ideas
- Electromagnetic waves can transfer energy without a medium.
- An electromagnetic wave transfers energy by means of changing electric and magnetic fields.
- Sometimes light acts as though it is a set of waves. Sometimes light acts as though it is a stream of particles.

Key Terms
electromagnetic wave
electromagnetic radiation
polarized light
photoelectric effect
photon

SECTION 2 — Waves of the Electromagnetic Spectrum

Key Ideas
- All electromagnetic waves travel at the same speed, but they have different wavelengths and different frequencies.
- The electromagnetic spectrum is made up of radio waves, infrared rays, visible light, ultraviolet rays, X-rays, and gamma rays.
- Radio waves and the Doppler effect can be used to tell the speeds of moving objects.
- The colors in the visible spectrum are red, orange, yellow, green, blue, and violet.

Key Terms
electromagnetic spectrum
radio wave
microwave
radar
magnetic resonance imaging
infrared ray
thermogram
visible light
ultraviolet ray
X-ray
gamma ray

SECTION 3 — Producing Visible Light

Key Ideas
- Light bulbs can be incandescent, fluorescent, neon, sodium vapor, or tungsten-halogen.
- Incandescent lights give off all the colors of the visible spectrum.
- Some organisms produce light by bioluminescence.

Key Terms
illuminated
luminous
spectroscope
incandescent light
fluorescent light
neon light
sodium vapor light
tungsten-halogen light
bioluminescence

SECTION 4 — Wireless Communication

INTEGRATING TECHNOLOGY

Key Ideas
- At broadcasting stations, music and speech are converted from sound into an electrical signal and then into a pattern of changes in a radio wave.
- AM broadcasts transmit information by modifying the amplitude of the signal while the frequency remains constant. FM broadcasts change the frequency of the signal while the amplitude remains constant.
- Cellular telephones transmit and receive signals using high-frequency radio waves.
- When you leave a message for a pager, the information is first sent to a receiving station. There it is coded and directed to the correct pager.
- Radio, television, and telephone signals are sent from Earth up to communications satellites, which then relay the signals to receivers around the world.

Key Terms
amplitude modulation
frequency modulation

USING THE INTERNET

ACTIVITY

www.science-explorer.phschool.com

CHAPTER 3 REVIEW

Reviewing Content

 For more review of key concepts, see the Interactive Student Tutorial CD-ROM.

Multiple Choice
Choose the letter of the best answer.

1. All electromagnetic waves have the same
   a. frequency.
   b. speed.
   c. wavelength.
   d. energy.
2. The electromagnetic waves with the longest wavelengths are
   a. radio waves.
   b. infrared rays.
   c. X-rays.
   d. gamma rays.
3. Which of the following does *not* belong in the electromagnetic spectrum?
   a. X-ray
   b. sound
   c. infrared ray
   d. radio wave
4. Light bulbs that glow when a filament inside them gets hot are called
   a. bioluminescent lights.
   b. fluorescent lights.
   c. incandescent lights.
   d. neon lights.
5. Television signals are transmitted by
   a. gamma rays.   b. infrared rays.
   c. X-rays.   d. radio waves.

True or False
If the statement is true, write true. If it is false, change the underlined word or words to make the statement true.

6. The photoelectric effect is evidence that light can act as a <u>particle</u>.
7. <u>Ultraviolet</u> rays can be felt as heat.
8. Fluorescent lights give off most of their energy as <u>infrared rays</u>.
9. A radio station is identified by the <u>amplitude</u> at which it broadcasts.
10. Radio and television transmitters can be placed on <u>satellites</u> and sent into orbit.

Checking Concepts

11. How do you know that electromagnetic waves can travel through a vacuum?
12. How does polarization show that light can act as a wave?
13. How is the Doppler effect used to find the speeds of moving objects?
14. Explain the difference between cellular telephones and cordless telephones.
15. A person lost in the woods at night may signal for help by turning a flashlight on and off according to a code known as Morse code. This is actually a modulated signal. Is it AM or FM? Explain your answer.
16. **Writing to Learn** Develop an advertising campaign to sell fluorescent lights. Your ad should describe two advantages of fluorescent lights over incandescent lights. Be sure to include a catchy slogan.

Thinking Visually

17. **Concept Map** Copy the concept map about electromagnetic waves onto a sheet of paper. Then complete it and add a title. (For more on concept maps, see the Skills Handbook.)

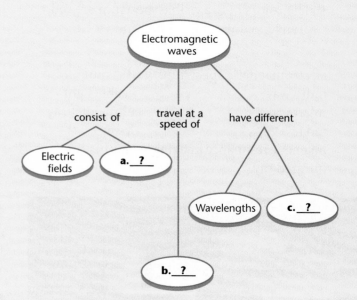

Applying Skills

The table below gives information about four radio stations. Use the table to answer Questions 18–20.

Call letters	Frequency
KLIZ	580 kHz
KMOM	103.7 MHz
WDAD	1030 kHz
WJFO	89.7 MHz

18. Interpreting Data Which radio station broadcasts at the longest wavelength? The shortest wavelength?

19. Classifying Which radio stations are AM? Which are FM?

20. Predicting You are going on a car trip across the United States. Which station would you expect to receive for the greater distance: KLIZ or KMOM?

Thinking Critically

21. Classifying List five examples of luminous objects and five examples of illuminated objects.

22. Relating Cause and Effect The waves of the electromagnetic spectrum that have the greatest frequency are also the most penetrating and can cause the most harm. Explain.

23. Applying Concepts What important information can be gathered from a thermogram of a house? How could this information be used to help save energy?

24. Comparing and Contrasting Make a table to compare the different types of wireless communication. Include headings such as: type of information transmitted; distance over which signal can be transmitted; one-way or two-way communication.

25. Problem Solving Suppose you are building an incubator for young chicks and need a source of heat. What type of light bulbs would you use? Explain.

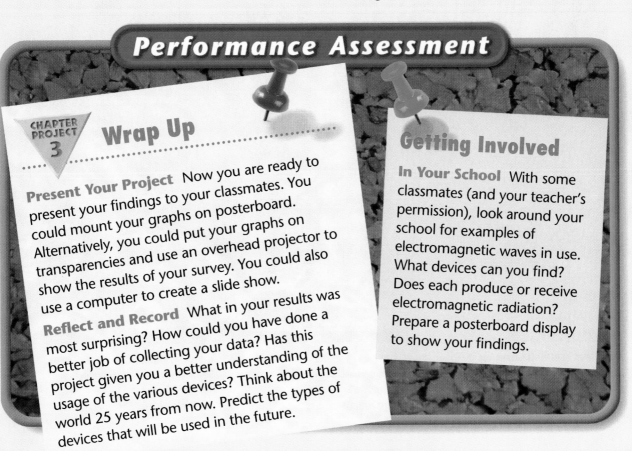

Performance Assessment

CHAPTER PROJECT 3 — Wrap Up

Present Your Project Now you are ready to present your findings to your classmates. You could mount your graphs on posterboard. Alternatively, you could put your graphs on transparencies and use an overhead projector to show the results of your survey. You could also use a computer to create a slide show.

Reflect and Record What in your results was most surprising? How could you have done a better job of collecting your data? Has this project given you a better understanding of the usage of the various devices? Think about the world 25 years from now. Predict the types of devices that will be used in the future.

Getting Involved

In Your School With some classmates (and your teacher's permission), look around your school for examples of electromagnetic waves in use. What devices can you find? Does each produce or receive electromagnetic radiation? Prepare a posterboard display to show your findings.

CHAPTER

4 Light

This kaleidoscope image is formed by two mirrors at right angles. Colored objects between the mirrors are reflected to form a repeated pattern.

WHAT'S AHEAD

What a Sight!

Look inside a kaleidoscope. Small beads or pieces of colored glass are reflected by mirrors, forming colorful, ever-changing patterns. Kaleidoscopes are optical instruments, devices that use arrangements of mirrors or lenses to produce images.

In this chapter, you will study how mirrors and lenses reflect and refract light. You will learn what causes the different colors of the objects all around you. You will use these ideas to create your own optical instrument.

Your Goal To construct an optical instrument that serves a specific purpose. It can be a kaleidoscope, a telescope, a periscope, a microscope, or something of your own creation.

To complete this project successfully you must
◆ design and build an optical instrument that includes at least one mirror or one lens
◆ demonstrate how your instrument works
◆ prepare a manual that explains the purpose of each part of your instrument

Get Started Begin to think about what you would like your optical instrument to do. Which would you like to see better—tiny objects or distant objects? Would you like to see around corners? Maybe you would prefer your instrument to produce striking images!

Check Your Progress You'll be working on this project as you study this chapter. To keep your project on track, look for Check Your Progress boxes at the following points.

Section 1 Review, page 116: Draw your optical instrument.
Section 3 Review, page 127: Build your optical instrument.
Section 5 Review, page 142: Test and modify your instrument. Prepare a manual explaining how your instrument works.

Wrap Up At the end of the chapter (page 145), you will demonstrate how your instrument works. You will also present your manual, showing the design and use of the instrument.

Integrating Life Science 🌐

SECTION 4 Seeing Light

Discover **Can You See Everything With One Eye?**
Try This **True Colors**

SECTION 5 Using Light

Discover **How Does a Pinhole Viewer Work?**
Try This **What a View!**

SECTION
① Reflection and Mirrors

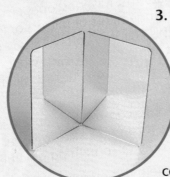

DISCOVER ••••••••••••••••••••••••••••••••••ACTIVITY••••

How Does Your Reflection Wink?

1. Look at your face in a mirror. Wink your right eye. Which eye does your reflection wink?

2. Tape two mirrors together so that they open and close like a book. Open them so they form a 90° angle with each other. **CAUTION:** *Be careful of any sharp edges.*

3. Looking into both mirrors at once, wink at your reflection again. Which eye does your reflection wink now?

Think It Over
Observing How does your reflection wink at you? How does the second reflection compare with the first reflection?

GUIDE FOR READING

◆ What happens when light strikes an object?

◆ What are the two kinds of reflection?

◆ What types of images are produced by plane, concave, and convex mirrors?

Reading Tip Before you read, preview the section and write down any new terms. As you read, find the meaning of each term.

Have you ever looked at a store window on a bright, sunny day? In order to see inside, you may have used your hands to block the glare. The glare is actually reflected light. The glare from the store window shows that glass can reflect light. But if you look at a clear glass window with no glare, you can see right through it.

When Light Strikes an Object

When light strikes an object, the light can be reflected, absorbed, or transmitted. Most objects reflect or absorb light. A material that reflects or absorbs all of the light that strikes it is **opaque** (oh PAYK). Most objects are opaque. You cannot see through opaque objects because light cannot pass through them. Examples of opaque materials include wood, metal, and cotton and wool fabrics.

A **transparent** material transmits light. When light strikes a transparent object, it passes right through, allowing you to see what is on the other side. Clear glass, water, and air are examples of transparent materials.

Other materials allow some light to pass through. This type of material is translucent. **Translucent** (trans LOO sunt) materials scatter light as it passes through. You can usually tell that there is something behind a translucent object, but you cannot see details clearly. Frosted glass and wax paper are translucent. Figure 1 shows opaque, transparent, and translucent objects.

◀ **Glare on a window**

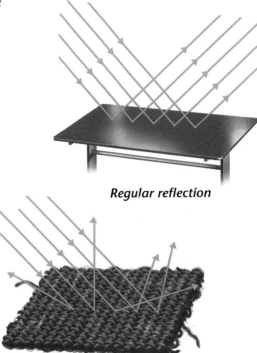

Figure 1 The spools of thread are opaque. They reflect light of various colors. The pitcher and glass are transparent. They transmit light, allowing you to see the milk inside. The leaf is translucent. The frog can be seen through the leaf but lacks detail.

Kinds of Reflection

When you look at some objects, such as a shiny metal fixture or a mirror, you can see yourself. But when you look at other objects, such as a book, a wooden table, or your pencil, you see only the object itself. **You can see most objects because light reflects, or bounces, off them.** What you see when you look at an object depends on how its surface reflects light.

Regular Reflection To show how light travels and reflects, you can represent light waves as straight lines called **rays.** Light rays reflect from a surface according to the law of reflection: the angle of reflection equals the angle of incidence.

Regular reflection occurs when parallel rays of light hit a smooth surface. All the rays are reflected at the same angle. For example, if you look at a sheet of shiny metal, you can see your own reflection. The light rays coming from you strike the smooth surface and are reflected regularly.

Diffuse Reflection When parallel rays of light hit a bumpy, or uneven, surface, **diffuse reflection** occurs. Each ray obeys the law of reflection. But since each ray hits the surface at a different angle, the rays are reflected at different angles. Because the reflected rays travel in all directions, diffuse reflection allows you to see an object from any position.

Most objects reflect light diffusely. This is because most objects do not have smooth surfaces. Even surfaces that appear to be smooth, such as a freshly painted wall, have small bumps that scatter light. If you look at a wall through a magnifying glass, you will see that the surface is not really smooth.

Regular reflection

Diffuse reflection

Figure 2 When light strikes a surface at an angle, it is reflected at the same angle. If the surface is smooth, the reflection is regular (top). If the surface is uneven, the reflection is diffuse (bottom).

Mirrors

Did you look in a mirror this morning? Maybe you combed your hair or brushed your teeth in front of a mirror. A mirror is a sheet of glass that has a smooth, silver-colored coating on one side. When light passes through the glass, the coating on the back reflects the light regularly, allowing you to see an image. An **image** is a copy of an object formed by reflected or refracted rays of light.

Mirrors can be flat or curved. The shape of the surface determines how the image will look. Depending on the shape of the mirror, the image can be the same size as the object, or it can be larger or smaller.

Plane Mirrors Look into a flat mirror, or **plane mirror.** You will see an image that is the same size as you are. Your image will seem to be the same distance behind the mirror as you are in front of it. **A plane mirror produces an image that is right-side up and the same size as the object being reflected.**

The image you see when you look in a plane mirror is a virtual image. **Virtual images** are right-side up, or upright. "Virtual" describes something that you can see, but does not really exist. You can't reach behind a mirror and touch your image.

Why do you see a virtual image? Figure 3 shows how the image of the dancer is formed by a plane mirror. Light rays reflected from the dancer travel out in all directions. They strike the mirror and are reflected toward the eye. The human brain assumes that light travels in a straight line. Even though the rays are reflected, the brain treats them as if they had come from behind the mirror. The dashed lines show the points from which the light rays appear to come. Since the dashed lines appear to come from behind the mirror, this is where the dancer's image appears to be located.

☑ *Checkpoint* What is a virtual image?

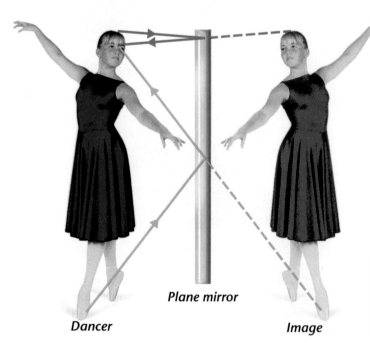

Plane mirror

Dancer

Image

Figure 3 A plane mirror forms a virtual image. When the dancer looks in the mirror, the rays of light from her body are reflected toward her. The rays appear to come from behind the mirror, where the image is formed.

Concave Mirrors A mirror with a surface that curves inward like the inside of a bowl is a **concave mirror.** Figure 4 shows how a concave mirror can reflect parallel rays of light so that they meet at a point. The point at which the rays meet is called the **focal point.**

Concave mirrors can form either virtual images or real images. The type of image formed by a concave mirror depends on the position of the object in relation to the focal point. Figure 5 shows how concave mirrors form images. If the object is farther away from the mirror than the focal point, the reflected rays form a real image. A **real image** is formed when rays actually meet at a point. Real images are upside down, or inverted. A real image may be larger or smaller than the object. If the object is between the focal point and the mirror, the image appears to be behind the mirror and is right-side up. Then it is a virtual image.

Some concave mirrors are used to project rays of light. For example, a car headlight has a bulb at the focal point of a concave mirror. When the light from the bulb spreads out and hits the mirror, the rays are reflected parallel to each other. This projects the light on the road ahead. Concave mirrors are also used to produce magnified images, as in makeup mirrors.

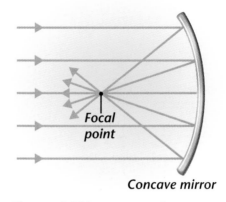

Figure 4 This concave mirror reflects parallel rays of light back through the focal point.

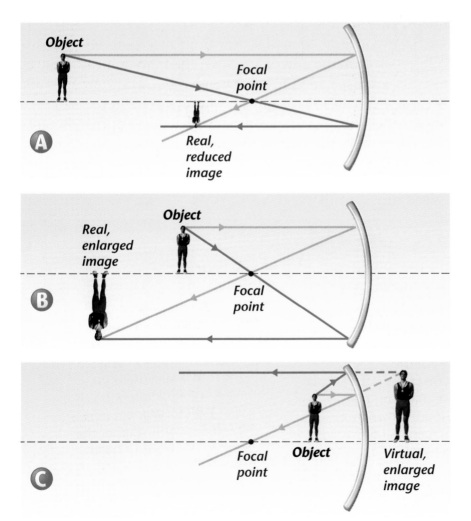

Figure 5 The type of image formed by a concave mirror depends on the position of the object in relation to the focal point. **A,B.** If the object is farther from the mirror than the focal point, the image is real and inverted. **C.** If the object is between the mirror and the focal point, the image is virtual and upright. *Interpreting Diagrams How can you tell that the images in A and B are real?*

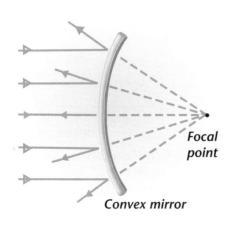

Focal point

Convex mirror

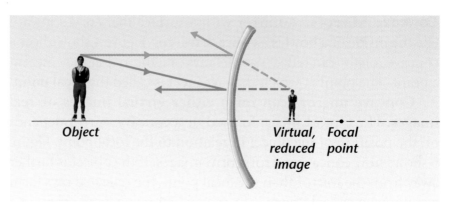

Object

Virtual, reduced image

Focal point

Figure 6 A convex mirror reflects parallel rays of light as though they came from the focal point behind the mirror. The image formed by a convex mirror is always virtual. *Applying Concepts* What is a convex mirror?

Convex Mirrors A mirror with a surface that curves outward is called a **convex mirror.** Figure 6 shows how some convex mirrors reflect parallel rays of light. The rays spread out but appear to come from a focal point behind the mirror. The focal point of a convex mirror is the point from which the rays appear to come. **Since the rays do not actually meet, images formed by convex mirrors are always virtual.**

Have you ever seen this warning on a rearview mirror? "Objects seen in the mirror are closer than they appear." Convex mirrors are used in cars as passenger-side rearview mirrors. Because a convex mirror spreads out rays of light, you can see a larger reflection area than you can with a plane mirror. Because you see more in the mirror, the images appear smaller and farther away than the objects themselves.

Section 1 Review

1. List four materials that are transparent, four that are translucent, and four that are opaque.
2. Describe two ways in which light can be reflected.
3. What types of images are produced by a plane mirror? A concave mirror? A convex mirror?
4. **Thinking Critically Applying Concepts**
   A slide projector projects an upright image onto a screen. The slides must be placed upside down in the projector. Is the image on the screen real or virtual? Give two reasons for your answer.

Check Your Progress
CHAPTER PROJECT 4
Decide on the purpose of your optical instrument. How will you use it? Draw and label a sketch of the optical instrument you would like to build. Will you use mirrors, lenses, or a combination of both? Show how your instrument affects light rays that enter it. Gather the materials you will need to build your instrument.

SECTION 2 Refraction and Lenses

How Can You Make an Image Appear on a Sheet of Paper?

1. Hold a hand lens about 2 meters from a window. Look through the lens. What do you see? **CAUTION:** *Do not look at the sun.*

2. Move the lens farther away from your eye. What changes do you notice?

3. Now hold the lens between the window and a sheet of paper, but closer to the paper. Slowly move the lens away from the paper and toward the window. Keep watching the paper. What do you see? What happens as you move the lens?

Think It Over

Observing How do you think an image is formed on a sheet of paper? Describe the image. Is it real or virtual? How do you know?

A fish tank can play tricks on your eyes. If you look through the side, the fish seems closer than if you look over the top. If you look through the corner, you may see the same fish twice. You see one image of the fish through the front of the tank and another image through the side of the tank. The two images appear in different places!

Refraction of Light

As you look into a fish tank, you are seeing the light bend as it passes through three different mediums. The mediums are the water, the glass of the tank, and the air. As the light passes from one medium to the next, it refracts. **When light rays enter a new medium at an angle, the change in speed causes them to bend, or change direction.**

Refraction can cause you to see something that may not actually be there. For example, refraction can form a mirage. It can also cause a beautiful sight, a rainbow.

GUIDE FOR READING

◆ What happens when light rays enter a medium at an angle?

◆ How do convex and concave lenses form images?

Reading Tip As you read, draw diagrams to show how each type of lens refracts light.

Figure 7 There is only one fish in this tank, but the refraction of light makes it look as though there are two.

Disappearing Glass

Try this activity 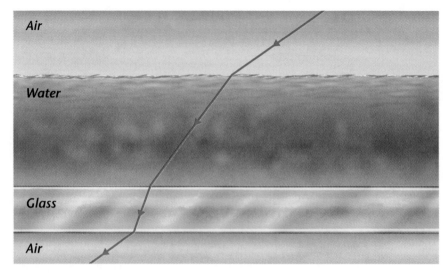 to see how different liquids refract light.

1. Place a small drinking glass inside a larger drinking glass. Can you see the small glass inside the larger one?

2. Fill both glasses with water. Look at the glasses from the side. Can you still see the smaller glass?

3. Empty and dry the glasses and refill them with vegetable oil. Describe what you see.

Inferring Why does the vegetable oil create a different effect than the water does?

Figure 8 As light passes from a less dense medium into a more dense medium, it slows down and is refracted. *Inferring Why does the light leaving the glass and entering air travel in its original direction?*

Index of Refraction Some mediums cause light to bend more than others. Figure 8 shows how light passes from air into water, from water into glass, and from glass into air again. When light passes from air into water, the light slows down. Light slows down even more when it passes from water into glass. Light travels fastest in air, a little slower in water, and slower still in glass. When light passes from glass back into air, the light speeds up. Notice that the ray that leaves the glass is traveling in the same direction as it was before it entered the water.

Glass causes light to bend more than either air or water because glass refracts light more. Another way to say this is that glass has a higher index of refraction than either air or water. A material's **index of refraction** is a measure of how much a ray of light bends when it enters that material. The higher the index of refraction of a medium, the more it bends light. The index of refraction of a vacuum is 1. The index of refraction of diamond is 2.42.

Figure 9 Passing white light through a prism causes the light to separate into its component colors. *Applying Concepts What determines the order in which the colors appear?*

Prisms Figure 9 shows that a beam of white light can be separated to show all the colors of the visible spectrum. Remember that white light is actually a mixture of many wavelengths of light, each with its own color. When white light enters a prism, each wavelength is refracted by a different amount. The longer the wavelength, the less the wave will be bent by a prism.

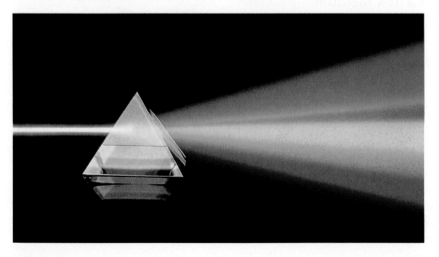

Rainbows When white light from the sun shines through tiny

drops of water, a rainbow may appear. Raindrops act like tiny prisms, refracting and reflecting the light and separating the colors. The colors of the rainbow always appear in the same order because raindrops refract the shorter wavelengths the most. Red, with the longest wavelength, is refracted the least. Violet, with the shortest wavelength, is refracted the most. The result is that white light is separated into the colors of the visible spectrum: red, orange, yellow, green, blue, and violet.

Mirages Imagine that you are in a car moving down a road on a hot, sunny day. The road ahead looks wet. Yet when you get there, the road is perfectly dry. Did the puddles disappear just before you got there? No, they were never there at all! What you saw was a mirage. A **mirage** (mih RAHJ) is an image of a distant object caused by refraction of light.

Figure 11 shows how a mirage forms. The air higher up is cooler than the air near the road. Light travels faster when it reaches the warmer air. As a result, the rays bend as they travel downward. Near the ground, the rays are traveling almost parallel to the ground but continue to bend until they begin to travel upward. As they travel upward they bend in the other direction. Your brain assumes that the rays have traveled in a straight line. They look just like rays reflected off a smooth surface, such as water. The observer sees a mirage.

☑ *Checkpoint* *What causes a mirage?*

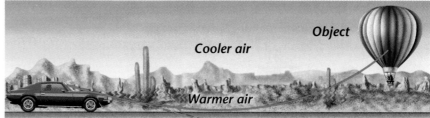

Figure 10 A rainbow forms when sunlight is refracted by tiny water droplets.

Figure 11 Light travels faster through hot air than through cool air. This causes light from the sky to curve as it approaches the ground. You see a mirage when refracted light appears to come from the ground.

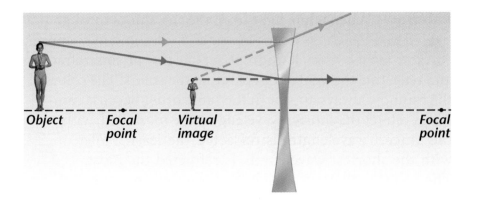

Figure 12 The ray that travels horizontally from the top of the object is refracted as though it is coming from the focal point on the same side of the lens as the object. The ray that travels toward the other focal point is refracted so it travels horizontally.
Interpreting Diagrams Why do the rays from a concave lens never meet?

Object   Focal point   Virtual image   Focal point

Lenses

Have you ever looked through binoculars, used a microscope or a camera, or worn eyeglasses? If so, you have used a lens to bend light. A **lens** is a curved piece of glass or other transparent material that is used to refract light. A lens forms an image by refracting light rays that pass through it. Like mirrors, lenses can have different shapes. The type of image formed by a lens depends on the shape of the lens.

Concave Lenses A **concave lens** is thinner in the center than at the edges. As parallel rays of light pass through a concave lens, they are bent away from the center of the lens. Figure 12 shows how the rays spread out, but appear to come from the focal point on the opposite side of the lens. **Because the light rays never meet, a concave lens can produce only a virtual image.**

Convex Lenses A **convex lens** is thicker in the center than at the edges. As parallel light rays pass through a convex lens, they are bent toward the center of the lens. The rays meet at the focal point of the lens and then continue on. The more curved the lens, the more it refracts light.

A convex lens acts somewhat like a concave mirror, because it focuses rays of light. **The type of image formed by a convex lens depends on the position of the object in relation to the focal point.** Figure 14 shows three examples. If the object is farther away than the focal point, the refracted rays form a real image on the other side of the lens. If the object is between the lens and the focal point, a virtual image forms on the same side of the lens as the object.

Concave lens

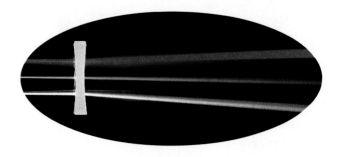

Convex lens

Figure 13 A concave lens refracts parallel rays of light so that they appear to come from one of the focal points. A convex lens refracts parallel rays of light so that they meet at the focal point.

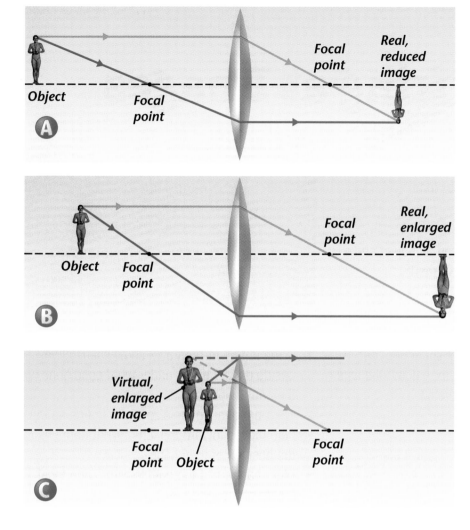

Figure 14 The type and size of image formed by a convex lens depend on the position of the object. **A, B.** If the object is farther from the focal point than the lens, the image is real and inverted. **C.** If the object is between the focal point and the lens, the image is virtual.

Section 2 Review

1. What happens to light rays as they pass from one medium into another medium?
2. What determines the type of image that is formed by a convex lens?
3. Why is it impossible for a concave lens to form a real image?
4. Explain why you sometimes see a rainbow during a rain shower or shortly afterward.
5. **Thinking Critically Problem Solving** Suppose you wanted to closely examine the leaf of a plant. Which type of lens would you use? Explain.

Science at Home

Here's how you can bend a pencil without touching it. Put a pencil in a glass of water, as shown in the photograph. Have your family members look at the pencil from the side. Using the idea of refraction, explain to your family why the pencil appears as it does.

Looking at Images

In this lab, you will control variables as you explore how images are formed by a convex lens.

Problem

How does the distance between an object and a convex lens affect the image formed?

Materials (per group)

tape
cardboard stand
light bulb and socket
battery and wires

convex lens
blank sheet of paper
clay, for holding the lens
meterstick

Procedure

1. Tape the paper onto the cardboard stand.
2. Place a lit bulb more than 2 m from the paper. Use the lens to focus light from the bulb onto the paper. Measure the distance from the lens to the paper. This is the approximate focal length of the lens you are using.
3. Copy the data table into your notebook.
4. Now place the bulb more than twice the focal length away from the lens. Record the position and size of the focused image on the paper. Measure the height of the bulb.
5. Now, move the bulb so that it is just over one focal length away from the lens. Record the position and size of the image.

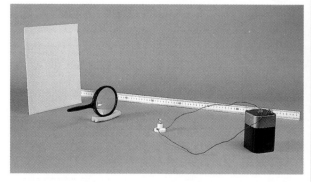

Analyze and Conclude

1. Is the image formed by a convex lens always upside down? If not, under what conditions is the image upright?
2. What happens to the size of the image as the bulb moves toward the lens? What happens to the position of the image?
3. What happens if the bulb is within one focal length of the lens? Explain.
4. **Think About It** Make a list of the variables in this experiment. Which variables did you keep constant? Which was the manipulated variable? Which was the responding variable?

Design an Experiment

With your teacher's approval and supervision, design an experiment to study images formed by convex lenses of various focal lengths. How does the focal length of the lens affect the position and size of the images produced?

DATA TABLE

Focal Length of Lens: _____ cm   Height of Bulb: _____ cm

Distance from Bulb to Lens (cm)	Image Position (upright or upside down)	Image Size (height in cm)

SECTION
3 Color

DISCOVER • ACTIVITY • • • •

How Do Colors Mix?

1. ✂ Carefully cut a disk with a diameter of about 10 cm out of a piece of sturdy white cardboard. Divide the disk into three equal-size segments. Use colored pencils to color one segment red, the next green, and the third blue.

2. Carefully punch two holes, about 2 cm apart, on opposite sides of the center of the disk.

3. Thread a string about 1 m long through the holes. Tie the ends of the string together so that the string forms a loop that passes through both holes.

4. With equal lengths of string on each side of the disk, turn the disk so that you are winding up the string. Predict what color(s) you will see if the disk spins fast.

5. Spin the disk by pulling and relaxing the string.

Think It Over

Observing What color do you see as the wheel spins fast? Was your prediction correct?

A s the morning sun slowly rises over the flower garden, the sunlight begins to reveal bright pink and orange poppies, purple pansies, and a striking display of many other colors. Each flower is beautiful, yet different. The light from the sun allows you to see each color clearly. But sunlight is white light. What makes each flower appear to be a different color?

The Color of Objects

The color of a flower depends on how it reflects light. Each flower absorbs some wavelengths of light and reflects other wavelengths. **You see an object as the color of the light it reflects.**

GUIDE FOR READING

◆ What determines the color of an object?

◆ What are the primary colors of light?

◆ How is mixing pigments different from mixing light?

Reading Tip Before you read, use the section headings to make an outline about color. Leave space to take notes as you read.

Objects in White Light Flowers and other objects reflect different colors of light. For example, when white light strikes the orange petals of a lily, the petals reflect mostly orange wavelengths. The petals absorb the other wavelengths. You see the petals as orange because orange wavelengths of light bounce off them and enter your eyes. On the other hand, the stem and leaves appear green. They reflect mostly green wavelengths and absorb the other colors.

What happens with black and white objects? A skunk looks black and white because some parts of it reflect all wavelengths of light while other parts do not reflect any light. When white light strikes the skunk's stripe, all the colors are reflected. The colors combine, so you see white light. When white light strikes the black parts of the skunk, all the light is absorbed and none is reflected. Your eyes see black.

Even colored and white objects can appear black if there is no light to reflect off them. Imagine being in a dark room. If there is no light present, then no light can reflect off the things in the room. No light enters your eyes, so you see nothing. If there is a small amount of light in the room, you may be able to make out the shapes of objects. However, you will not be able to tell their colors.

Objects in Colored Light Objects can look a different color depending on the color of light in which they are seen. Figure 17 shows two photographs of a desktop, each taken under different light. The first picture was taken under ordinary white light. In it, the keyboard is blue and the folder is red. The second picture was taken under green light. When green light shines on an object,

Figure 15 The petals of this lily appear orange because they reflect orange light. The stems and leaves appear green because they reflect green light.

Figure 16 The white part of this skunk reflects all colors of light. *Applying Concepts Why do the skunk's legs look black?*

Figure 17 In white light, objects appear in many different colors (left). If viewed under green light, the same objects appear in shades of green or black (right). *Predicting How would these objects look under blue light?*

the object either reflects or absorbs the green light. Since red and blue objects reflect only red and blue light, they absorb all of the green light. The binder looks black.

Objects Seen Through Filters Some transparent materials allow only certain colors of light to pass through them. They reflect or absorb the other colors. Such materials are called color filters. For example, a red filter is a piece of glass or plastic that allows only red light to pass through. Spotlights on theater stages often use color filters to produce different color effects. Photographic slides are color filters, too. A slide projector shines white light through a combination of color filters. The image you see on the screen shows the colors that each part of the slide allows through.

☑ Checkpoint *What is a color filter?*

Combining Colors

An understanding of color is very useful in photography, art, theater lighting, and printing. People who work with color must know how to produce a wide range of colors from just a few basic colors. It is possible to produce any color by mixing colors of the spectrum in varying amounts. Three colors that can be used to make any other color are called **primary colors.** Any two primary colors combined in equal amounts produce a **secondary color.**

Mixing Colors of Light **The primary colors of light are red, green, and blue. When combined in equal amounts, the primary colors produce white light.** But if they are combined in varying amounts, they can produce any other color. For example, red and green combine to form yellow light. Yellow is a secondary color of light because it is produced from two primary colors.

Sharpen your Skills

Developing Hypotheses

ACTIVITY

1. Carefully make a color wheel with eight segments. Use colored pencils to color alternate blue and yellow segments.

2. Predict what color you will see if you spin the wheel. Write a hypothesis of what you think the outcome will be. Be sure to write your hypothesis as an *"If . . . then . . ."* statement.

3. Spin the wheel. What do you see? Does it confirm your hypothesis?

4. Repeat the activity with color wheels that have different pairs of colors.

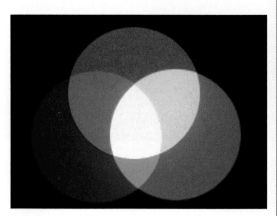

Primary colors of light

Figure 18 The primary colors of light are red, green, and blue. When combined in equal amounts, the primary colors of light form white light. A color television produces all colors of light by combining red, green, and blue light in varying amounts. *Interpreting Photographs How does a television show black?*

Visual Arts
CONNECTION

Ever since the first cave artists painted about 20,000 years ago, pigments made from natural materials have been used to create pictures. In the 1400s, Renaissance painters such as Leonardo da Vinci and Raphael used many more colorful pigments to create their vivid paintings. Pigments were derived from minerals, plants, and animals.

In Your Journal

Look at the color names for markers, paints, or crayons. Do you see vermilion (red), azure (blue) or ochre (brown)? These colors were all originally made from minerals. Now these colors are made from chemicals. Can you find the names of other colors that may have originally come from minerals?

The secondary colors of light are yellow (red + green), cyan (green + blue), and magenta (red + blue). Figure 18 shows the primary colors of light.

A primary color and a secondary color can combine to make white. Any two colors that combine to form white light are called **complementary colors.** Yellow and blue are complementary colors, as are cyan and red, and magenta and green.

INTEGRATING TECHNOLOGY A color television screen produces only three colors of light. Figure 18 shows a magnified portion of a color television screen. Notice that the picture on the screen is made up of little groups of red, green, and blue lights. By varying the brightness of each colored light, the television produces pictures of many different colors.

Mixing Pigments How do artists produce the many shades of colors you see in paintings? Paints and dyes have different colors because of the pigments they contain. **Pigments** are substances that are used to color other materials. Color pigments are opaque substances that reflect particular colors. The color you see is the color that particular pigment reflects.

Mixing colors of pigments is different from mixing colors of light. **As pigments are added together, fewer colors of light are reflected and more are absorbed.** The more pigments that are combined, the darker the mixture looks.

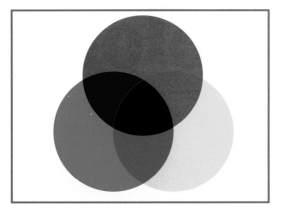

Primary colors of pigments

Figure 19 The primary colors of pigments are cyan, yellow, and magenta (left). The photograph shows an enlargement of a printed page. Four-color printing uses the three primary colors of pigment, plus black.

The primary colors of pigments are cyan, yellow, and magenta. If you combine all three primary colors of pigments in equal amounts, you get black. If you combine two primary colors of pigments in equal amounts, you get a secondary color. The secondary colors of pigments are red (magenta + yellow), green (cyan + yellow), and blue (magenta + cyan). By combining pigments in varying amounts, you can produce any other color. Figure 19 shows the primary colors of pigments.

If you use a magnifying glass to look at color pictures in this book, you will see that the pictures are made up of tiny dots of different colors of ink. The colors used are cyan, yellow, and magenta. Black ink is also used to make pictures darker. Because of the four colors of ink used, the process that produced this book is called four-color printing.

Section 3 Review

1. Why do objects have different colors?
2. What are the primary colors of light? What happens when the primary colors of light are mixed in equal amounts?
3. What happens when the primary colors of pigments are mixed in equal amounts?
4. What colors are used in the four-color printing process?
5. **Thinking Critically Comparing and Contrasting** Make a table that compares and contrasts the primary and secondary colors of light and those of pigments.

Check Your Progress

CHAPTER PROJECT 4

Build your optical instrument according to the sketch you prepared. How does your instrument use reflection or refraction to produce and clarify images? Do you need to be able to change the focus of the image? Does your instrument have moving parts? How will you combine the different parts of the instrument?

Changing Colors

Stage lighting in theaters uses color filters to control the colors of light on stage. In this lab you will study the effect of color filters on white light.

Skills Focus

observing, predicting, inferring

Materials (per group)

shoe box
flashlight
scissors
removable tape
red object (such as a ripe tomato)
yellow object (such as a ripe lemon)
blue object (such as blue construction paper)
red, green, and blue cellophane, enough to cover the top of the shoe box

Procedure

1. Carefully cut a large rectangular hole in the lid of the shoe box. The hole should be just a little smaller than the lid of the box.
2. Carefully cut a small, round hole in the center of one of the ends of the shoe box.
3. Tape the red cellophane under the lid of the shoe box, covering the hole in the lid.
4. Place the objects in the box and put the lid on.
5. In a darkened room, shine the flashlight into the shoe box through the side hole. Note the apparent color of each object in the box.
6. Repeat Steps 3–5 using the other colors of cellophane.

Analyze and Conclude

1. What did you see when you looked through the red cellophane? Explain why each object appeared as it did.
2. What did you see when you looked through the blue cellophane? Explain.
3. What color of light does each piece of cellophane allow through?
4. Predict what you would see under each piece of cellophane if you put a white object in the box. Test your prediction.
5. Use diagrams to show how each color of cellophane affects the white light from the flashlight.
6. **Think About It** Do color filters work more like pigments or like colors of light? What would happen if you shined a flashlight through both a red and a green filter? Explain.

Getting Involved

Visit a local theater or talk to a lighting designer to find out how color filters are used to produce different stage effects.

SECTION 4 Seeing Light

DISCOVER

Can You See Everything With One Eye?

1. Write an X and an O on a sheet of paper. They should be about 5 cm apart.
2. Hold the sheet of paper at arm's length.
3. Close or cover your left eye. Stare at the X with your right eye.
4. Slowly move the paper toward your face while staring at the X. What do you notice?
5. Repeat the activity, keeping both eyes open. What difference do you notice?

Think It Over

Posing Questions Write two questions about vision that you could investigate using the X and the O.

---

he excitement mounts as the pitcher goes into his windup. As he goes through his motion, he keeps his eye on the strike zone. The batter watches the pitcher release the ball, then swings. Crack! The batter strikes the ball, drops the bat, and sprints toward first base. From your seat behind home plate, you watch the ball travel toward the outfield. Will it be a base hit? The left fielder watches the ball leave the bat and travel toward him. It goes over his head—a two-base hit!

Everyone involved has been following the first rule of baseball: Keep your eye on the ball. As the ball moves, the eyes must adjust continuously to keep it in focus. Fortunately, this change in focus happens automatically.

GUIDE FOR READING

◆ How do your eyes allow you to see?

◆ What kind of lenses are used to correct vision problems?

Reading Tip As you read, make a flowchart that shows how light travels through the eye and how the brain interprets the image.

Figure 20 As the ball moves through the air, your eyes must continuously adjust their focus to see the ball.

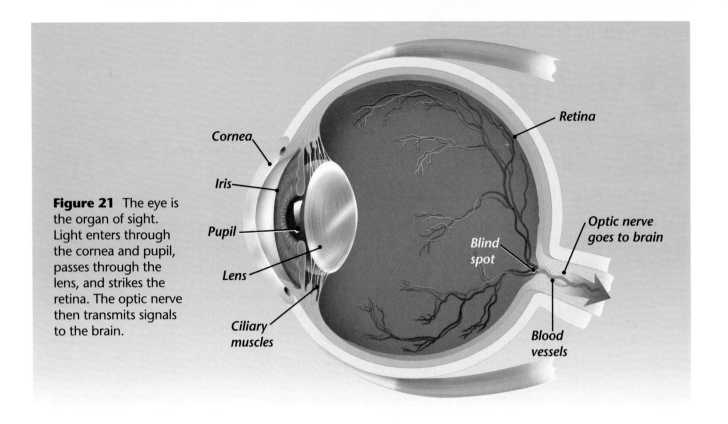

Cornea

Iris

Pupil

Lens

Ciliary muscles

Retina

Blind spot

Optic nerve goes to brain

Blood vessels

Figure 21 The eye is the organ of sight. Light enters through the cornea and pupil, passes through the lens, and strikes the retina. The optic nerve then transmits signals to the brain.

The Human Eye

Your eyes are complicated organs, with each part playing its own role in helping you see. **You see objects because of a series of steps that involve the structures of the eye and the brain.**

The Cornea Light enters the eye through the transparent front surface called the **cornea.** The cornea protects the eye from dust. It also acts as a lens, bending rays of light as they enter the eye. Each time you blink, your eyelids act like little windshield wipers, cleansing and moistening the cornea.

The Iris The **iris** is a ring of muscle that contracts and expands to change the amount of light that enters the eye. The iris gives the eye its color. In most people the iris is brown; in others it is blue or green.

The Pupil The **pupil** is the part of the eye that looks black. It is actually a hole, covered by the clear cornea. The pupil looks black because it is an opening into the dark inside of the eye. Figure 22 shows how the size of the pupil depends on whether the iris is contracted or expanded. In dim light, the pupil becomes larger, allowing more light in. In very bright light, the pupil becomes smaller, reducing the amount of light that enters the eye.

Figure 22 In dim light, the iris contracts. The pupil gets bigger and allows more light into the eye. *Relating Cause and Effect What happens in bright light?*

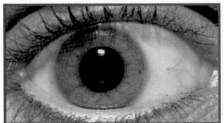

The Lens Just behind the pupil is the lens. The lens of your eye is a convex lens. The lens refracts light, forming an image on the lining of your eyeball. Figure 23 shows how the lens changes its focus. When you focus on a distant object, the ciliary muscles holding the lens contract, making the lens longer and thinner. When you focus on a nearby object, the muscles relax and the lens becomes shorter and fatter.

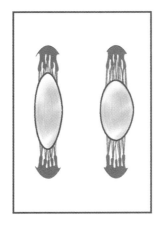

Figure 23 The ciliary muscles holding the lens in place contract to lengthen the lens. The muscles relax to shorten the lens.

The Retina The layer of cells lining the inside of the eyeball is the **retina.** As the cornea and the lens refract light, an upside-down image is formed on the retina. The retina is made up of millions of tiny, light-sensitive cells called rods and cones. The rods and cones generate small nerve signals when they are hit by light.

The **rods** contain a pigment that reacts to small amounts of light. The rods distinguish among black, white, and shades of gray. They allow you to see in dim light, so they are important for night vision.

The **cones** respond to colors. There are three types of cones: those that detect red light, those that detect green light, and those that detect blue light. The cone cells only function in bright light. This is why it is difficult to distinguish colors in dim light.

The Optic Nerve and the Brain The signals generated by the rods and cones travel to your brain along a short, thick nerve called the **optic nerve.** When the signals reach your brain, it automatically turns the image right-side up. Your brain also combines the two images, one from each eye, into a single three-dimensional image.

There is one spot on the retina that does not have any rods or cones. This blind spot is the part of the retina where the optic nerve begins. You cannot see light that falls on the blind spot. However, an object whose light falls on the blind spot of one eye can usually be seen with the other eye. If you keep both eyes open, you do not notice the effect of the blind spots.

✓ *Checkpoint* *Where in the eye is the image formed?*

Correcting Vision

In some people, the eyeball is slightly too long or too short, so the image on the retina is slightly out of focus. Fortunately, wearing glasses or contact lenses can usually correct this type of vision problem. **Some lenses in eyeglasses are convex and some are concave. The type of lens used depends on whether the eyeball is too long or too short.**

True Colors ACTIVITY

When you stare too long at a color, the cones in your eyes get tired.

1. Stare at the bottom right star of the flag for at least 60 seconds. Do not move your eyes or blink during that time.

2. Now stare at a sheet of blank white paper.

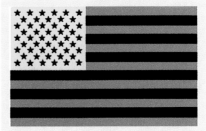

Observing What do you see when you look at the white paper? How are the colors you see related to the colors in the original art?

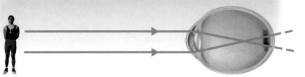

Nearsightedness (eyeball too long)

Image forms in front of retina

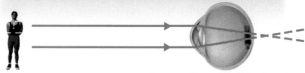

Farsightedness (eyeball too short)

Image forms behind retina

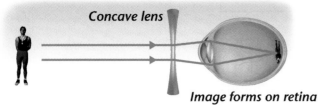

Correction

Concave lens

Image forms on retina

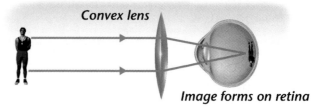

Correction

Convex lens

Image forms on retina

Figure 24 Nearsightedness and farsightedness are caused when the eyeball is a little too long or too short. Both can be corrected by wearing lenses.

Nearsightedness A **nearsighted** person can see nearby things clearly, but objects at a distance appear blurry. This happens because the eyeball is a little too long. The lens focuses the image in front of the retina. A nearsighted person can wear eyeglasses with concave lenses to see more clearly. A concave lens spreads out the rays a little before they enter the lens of the eye. This causes the image to form a little farther back, on the retina.

Farsightedness A **farsighted** person can see distant objects, but nearby objects appear blurry. This happens when the eyeball is a little too short. The lens focuses the rays of light so that they would meet behind the retina. The image that falls on the retina is out of focus. A farsighted person can wear glasses with convex lenses. A convex lens makes the rays bend toward each other a little before they enter the eye. A clear image is then formed on the retina.

Section 4 Review

1. Describe briefly the function of each of these structures in allowing a person to see: the cornea, pupil, lens, retina, optic nerve, brain.
2. How and why does the pupil change size?
3. What causes nearsightedness? Farsightedness? How can each be corrected?
4. **Thinking Critically Comparing and Contrasting** Compare and contrast the functions of the rods and the cones.

Science at Home

Roll a sheet of paper into a tube and hold one end up to your right eye. Hold your left hand against the left side of the far end of the tube with your palm facing toward you. Keeping both eyes open, look at a distant object. Draw and label a diagram of what you see. What do you think causes this optical illusion?

How Does a Pinhole Viewer Work?

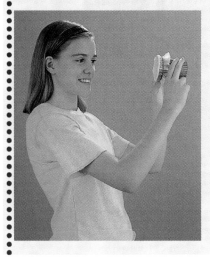

1. ✂ Carefully use a pin to make a tiny hole in the center of the bottom of a paper cup.

2. Place a piece of wax paper over the open end of the cup. Hold the paper in place with a rubber band.

3. Turn off the room lights. Point the end of the cup with the hole in it at a bright window. **CAUTION:** *Do not look directly at the sun.*

4. Look at the image formed on the wax paper.

Think It Over
Classifying Describe the image you see. Is it upside down or right-side up? Is it smaller or larger than the actual object? What type of image is it?

Have you ever seen photos of the moons of Jupiter? Have you ever thought it would be exciting to fly close to the rings of Saturn? Of course you know that traveling in space has been done for only a few decades. But you might be surprised to know that the moons of Jupiter and the rings of Saturn had not been seen by anyone before the year 1600. It was only about 1609 that a new invention, the telescope, made those objects visible to people on Earth.

Since the 1600s, astronomers have built more powerful telescopes that allow them to see objects in space that are very far from Earth. The Trifid Nebula, for example, is a cloud of gas and dust in space 28,380 trillion kilometers from Earth. It took about 3,000 years for light from this nebula to travel to Earth.

In this section you will learn how simple a device the telescope is. You may wonder why no one invented it sooner!

GUIDE FOR READING

◆ How do telescopes and microscopes work?

◆ How does a camera work?

◆ How is laser light different from ordinary light?

Reading Tip Before you read, preview the section to identify devices that use light. As you read, make notes about how each device is commonly used.

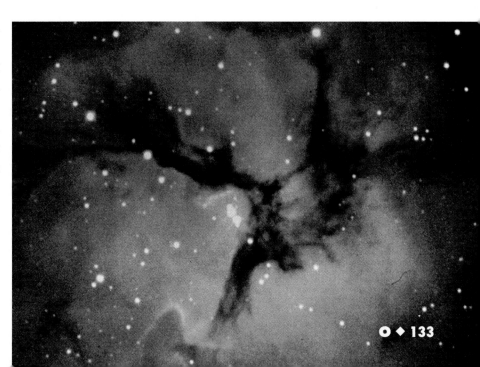

The Trifid Nebula ▶

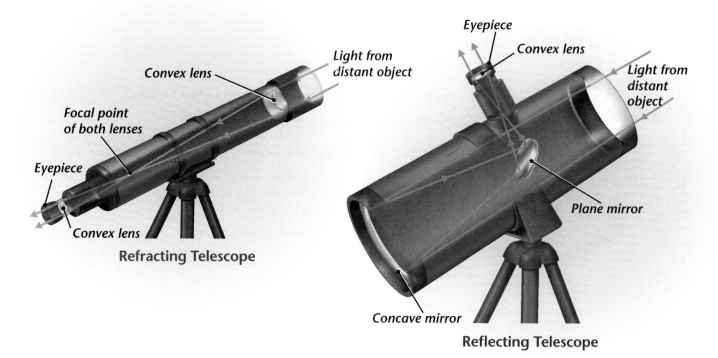

Refracting Telescope

Reflecting Telescope

Figure 25 A refracting telescope (left) uses a combination of lenses to form an image. A reflecting telescope (right) uses a combination of lenses and mirrors to form an image.

What a View!

You can use two hand lenses of different strengths to form an image.

1. Hold the stronger lens close to your eye.
2. Hold the other lens at arm's length.
3. Use your lens combination to view a distant object.
CAUTION: *Do not look at the sun.* Adjust the distance of the farther lens until the image is clear.

Classifying What type of image do you see? What type of telescope is similar to this lens combination?

Telescopes

Distant objects are difficult to see because light from them has spread out by the time it reaches your eyes. Your eyes are too small to gather much light. A **telescope** forms enlarged images of distant objects. **Telescopes use lenses or mirrors to collect and focus light from distant objects.** The most common use of telescopes is to collect light from space. This allows astronomers to see objects they could not see with their eyes alone.

There are two main types of telescopes: refracting telescopes and reflecting telescopes. Both types are shown in Figure 25. A **refracting telescope** consists of two convex lenses, one at each end of a long tube. The larger lens is the objective lens. The **objective lens** gathers the light coming from an object and focuses the rays to form a real image. The lens close to your eye is the eyepiece lens. The **eyepiece lens** magnifies the image so you can see it clearly. The image you see through a refracting telescope is upside down.

A **reflecting telescope** uses a large concave mirror to gather light. The mirror collects light from distant objects and focuses the rays to form a real image. A small mirror inside the telescope reflects the image to the eyepiece lens. The eyepiece can be replaced by a camera to record the image. The image you see through a reflecting telescope is upside down also.

✓ *Checkpoint* What are the two main types of telescopes?

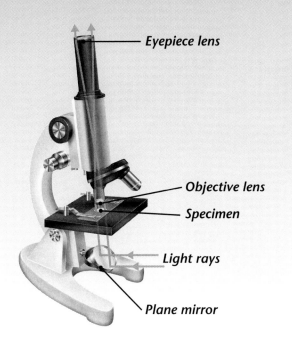

Eyepiece lens

Objective lens

Specimen

Light rays

Plane mirror

Figure 26 A microscope uses a combination of lenses to form enlarged images of tiny objects. You can use a microscope to look at microorganisms such as these single-celled algae.

Microscopes

What would happen if you used a telescope to look at small objects close up? The principle of a refracting telescope can also be used to enlarge very small objects. A **microscope** forms enlarged images of tiny objects. **A microscope uses a combination of lenses to produce and magnify an image.**

Figure 26 shows how a microscope works. The specimen to be viewed is placed on a glass or plastic slide and covered with a coverslip. The slide is then placed on the platform of the microscope. A light source or a mirror illuminates the slide from below. The objective lens, placed very close to the slide, forms a real, but enlarged, image of the tiny object. The eyepiece lens enlarges the image even more. The image can be hundreds of times larger than the object itself. Most microscopes have two or three objective lenses so you can change the magnifying power.

Cameras

A **camera** uses lenses to focus light and record an image of an object. Cameras range from simple pinhole cameras to high-tech models used by professional photographers. They all work in basically the same way.

In a pinhole camera, rays of light from an object enter a small box through a tiny pinhole. This light forms an upside down, real image on the back of the box. However, most cameras are more complex.

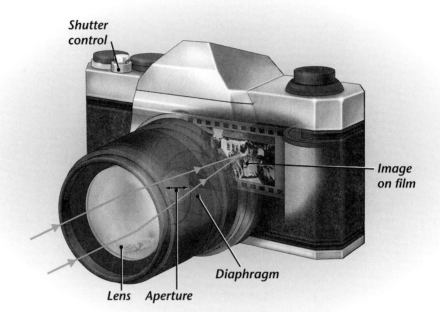

Shutter control

Image on film

Diaphragm

Lens   Aperture

Figure 27 A camera uses a lens to project an image onto film. *Comparing and Contrasting Compare the lens, diaphragm, aperture, and film of the camera to the corresponding parts of the eye.*

Figure 27 shows the structure of a camera. The shutter is a little door behind an aperture, or hole. **When you press the button of a camera to take a photograph, you briefly open the shutter. This allows light to hit the film.** The shutter speed is the amount of time the shutter is open, or the exposure time. The diaphragm controls the amount of light that enters the camera by changing the size of the aperture. This is similar to the way that the iris of your eye controls the amount of light that enters your eye through the pupil.

Inside the camera, light passes through a convex lens or a combination of lenses. The lens focuses the light to form a real image on the film. To get a clear, properly focused image, the lens must move closer to or away from the film, depending on whether the object is close or far away. Most cameras allow you to move the lens by turning a ring on the front of the camera. An automatic camera moves the lens itself until the image is focused.

Photographic film is a material that undergoes a chemical change when exposed to light. The film is developed into negatives by treating it with chemicals. The negative is used to print the image on paper. The result is a photograph.

☑ *Checkpoint* *What part of a camera controls the amount of light that enters the camera?*

Lasers

In a laser show, thin beams of light flash across the walls and ceiling. These are not ordinary beams of light. The light can be focused into a narrow beam with very little spread. It can produce a clear, sharp image on a flat surface. The properties of these beams of light allow them to have many different uses.

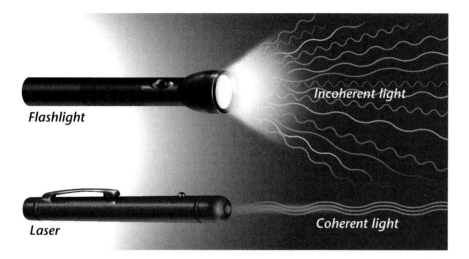

Figure 28 White light is made up of many different wavelengths, or colors. Laser light consists of light of only one wavelength. All the crests of laser light are in step with each other.

When you turn on an ordinary light bulb, the light spreads out and is visible around the room. Ordinary white light is made up of light of many different colors and wavelengths. **A laser beam consists of waves that all have the same wavelength, or color. The waves are coherent, or in step.** All the crests of the waves align with each other, as do all the troughs.

The word **laser** comes from the first letters of the words that describe how it works: **l**ight **a**mplification by **s**timulated **e**mission of **r**adiation. *Light amplification* means that the light is strengthened, or given more energy. *Stimulated emission* means that the atoms emit light when exposed to radiation.

A laser consists of a tube that contains a material such as ruby or a helium-neon mixture. The material used determines the wavelength and intensity of the light produced.

Electricity, a light flash, or a chemical reaction causes the material in the tube to emit light. The light travels up and down the tube. One end of the tube is covered with a mirror. This mirror reflects all the photons that hit it. The photons then travel to a partially reflecting mirror at the other end of the tube. As the photons travel in the tube, they bump into other atoms. The atoms then emit more photons with the same amount of energy as the one that caused the collision. The photons then travel together in step with each other. This process continues until there is a stream of in-step photons traveling up and down the tube. Some of the light "leaks" through the partially reflecting mirror. The light that comes out of the tube is the laser beam.

Figure 29 This diagram of a ruby laser shows photons moving up and down the tube. The light that comes out of the tube is the laser beam.

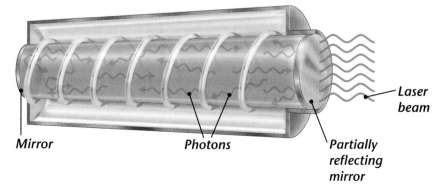

Uses of Lasers

Lasers have many practical applications. Lasers are widely used by surveyors and engineers. A laser beam is so straight that it can be used to make sure that surfaces are level and that bridges and tunnels are properly aligned. For example, a laser beam was used to guide the tunnel diggers who dug the Channel Tunnel between England and France. Some very powerful lasers can even cut through steel. Many stores and supermarkets use lasers. A laser scans the universal product code, or bar code. The store's computer then displays the price of the object.

Compact Discs Lasers can be used to store and read information. A compact disc is produced by converting data into electrical signals. The electrical signals are converted to a laser beam, which cuts a pattern of pits on a blank disc. When you play a compact disc or read one with a computer, a laser beam shines on the surface and is reflected. The reflection patterns vary because

SCIENCE & History

Optical Instruments

The development of optical instruments has changed the way we look at the world and beyond. It has allowed major scientific discoveries.

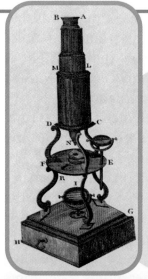

1595 THE NETHERLANDS
Microscopes

The first useful microscope is thought to have been constructed by Zacharias Jansen or his father, Hans. The Jansen microscope could magnify images up to nine times the size of the object. By the mid-1600s, microscopes looked like the one shown.

| 1300 | 1400 | 1500 | 1600 |

1350 ITALY
Spectacles

Craftsmen made small disks of glass that could be framed and worn in front of the eyes. Early spectacles consisted of convex lenses. They were used as reading glasses.

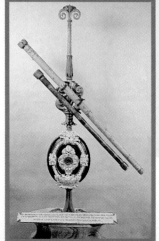

1607 THE NETHERLANDS
Telescopes

The first telescope was made of two convex lenses. It was from this simple invention that the Italian scientist Galileo developed his more powerful telescopes.

of the pits. The compact disc player or disc drive changes these patterns into electrical signals. The signals are sent to speakers and you hear sound.

Surgery   Doctors can use lasers instead of scalpels to make
 **INTEGRATING HEALTH** incisions. The beam of light can be powerful enough to cut through flesh. As the laser makes the incision, it seals the cut blood vessels. This reduces the amount of blood a patient loses. Laser incisions usually heal faster than scalpel cuts, so the patient's recovery time is reduced.

Eye doctors use lasers to repair detached retinas. If the retina falls away from the inside of the eye, the rods and cones can no longer send signals to the brain. This can lead to total or partial blindness. The doctor can use a laser to "weld" or burn the retina back onto the eyeball. Lasers can also be used to destroy or remove skin blemishes and cancerous growths.

In Your Journal

Find out more about early photography and people's reactions to it. Then imagine you are an early photographer explaining photography to someone who has never seen a photo. Create a two-page dialog in which you answer that person's questions on the process and possible uses of photography.

1990 UNITED STATES

Hubble Space Telescope

This large reflecting telescope was launched by the crew of the space shuttle *Discovery*. It can detect infrared, visible, and ultraviolet rays in space and send pictures back to Earth.

1700	1800	1900	2000

1826 FRANCE

Cameras

The earliest camera, the pinhole camera, was adapted to form and record permanent images by Joseph Nicéphore Niepce and Louis-Jacques-Mandé Daguerre of France. This is one of Nicéphore Niepce's earliest photographic images.

1960 UNITED STATES

Lasers

The first laser, built by American Theodore Maiman, used a rod of ruby to produce light. Since then, lasers have been used in numerous ways, including engineering, medicine, and communications.

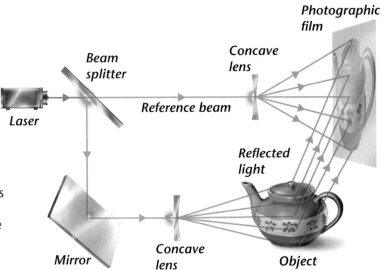

Figure 30 To form a hologram, the light from a laser is split into two beams. When the two beams strike the photographic film, an interference pattern produces the image, or hologram.

Holography Check out your local video store or newsstand. Some videos and magazines have pictures that appear to move as you walk by. A **hologram** is a three-dimensional photograph created by using the light from a laser. The process is called holography.

Figure 30 shows how a hologram is produced. A laser beam is split into two beams. One beam passes through a concave lens, behind which is a piece of photographic film. The concave lens spreads out the rays of light before they hit the film. The second beam is sent to a mirror and reflected toward another concave lens, behind which is the object being photographed. Again, the rays are spread out by the lens before they hit the object. The object then reflects these rays toward the film, where they interfere with rays from the first beam. The interference pattern between the two beams of light creates a three-dimensional image that is recorded on the film.

✓ *Checkpoint* **What are four uses of lasers?**

Figure 31 Optical fibers are thin strands of glass or plastic that carry light.

Optical Fibers

Lasers are also used in communications. A laser beam is electromagnetic radiation of a single wavelength. It is similar to radio waves and so can carry signals by modulation. Unlike radio waves, laser beams are not usually sent through the air. Instead, they are sent through optical fibers. **Optical fibers** are long, thin strands of glass or plastic that can carry light for long distances without allowing the light to fade out. You may have seen optical fibers in lamps or in the small hand-held lights that are sometimes sold at circuses and other shows.

EXPLORING Uses of Lasers

The invention of the laser has led to many developments in technology and communication.

A laser beam reads ▲ information from tiny pits on a compact disc.

▲ Civil engineers use laser beams to ensure that buildings are straight.

▼ Optical fibers carry beams of laser light great distances. One tiny fiber can carry thousands more phone conversations than the traditional copper wire cable.

▲ A supermarket scanner reflects a laser off a set of lines known as a universal product code, or UPC. Each product has a unique code. This code represents a number that is programmed into the store's computer. The computer then displays the name of the object and the price on a screen near the cash register.

Small, hand-held lasers are commonly used as pointers in lectures and presentations.

◀ Banks now commonly put small holograms on credit cards for security reasons. The hologram makes credit cards difficult to copy.

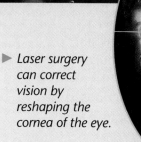

▶ Laser surgery can correct vision by reshaping the cornea of the eye.

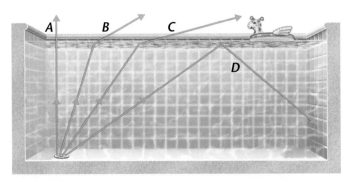

Figure 32 The angle of the light beam determines whether or not the light can leave the medium. If the angle is great enough, the light is reflected back into the water.

Figure 32 shows how the light can stay inside a medium and not pass through the surface to the outside. When a light beam hits a surface at a 0° angle of incidence, it goes through the surface without being bent. As the angle of incidence gets larger, the light is bent more and more. When it travels nearly parallel to the surface, all of the light is reflected. This complete reflection of light by the inside surface of a medium is called **total internal reflection.** Figure 33 shows how a laser beam reflects off the inside of an optical fiber and keeps going, even if the optical fiber is curved or curled up.

Communications To send signals through optical fibers, the electrical signals that start out over copper wires are changed into pulses of light by tiny lasers. Then the signals can travel over long ranges in the optical fiber. Optical fibers have led to great improvements in telephone service, computer networks, and cable television systems. Signals sent over optical fibers are usually faster and clearer than those sent over copper wire. One tiny optical fiber can carry thousands of phone conversations at the same time. Optical fibers are so much thinner than copper wire that more fibers can be placed in the same space underground.

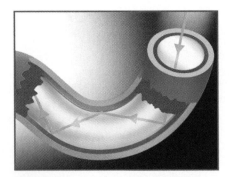

Figure 33 Light travels through an optical fiber by total internal reflection.

Medicine Optical fibers are commonly used in medical instruments. Doctors can insert a thin optical fiber inside various parts of the body, such as the heart or the stomach. The optical fiber can be attached to a microscope or a camera. In this way, doctors can examine internal organs without having to perform surgery.

Section 5 Review

1. Compare and contrast refracting telescopes and reflecting telescopes.
2. How does a microscope work?
3. Why does a camera produce an upside-down image?
4. What is a laser beam composed of?
5. Describe two uses of optical fibers.
6. **Thinking Critically Making Judgments** Do you think it would be dangerous to look into a laser beam? Explain your answer.

Check Your Progress CHAPTER PROJECT 4
Now it is time to test your optical instrument. Does it work as you designed it to? Can you adjust the mirror or lenses to change the focus of the image? Do moving parts move smoothly and easily? Modify any parts of your instrument to help it work better. Prepare a manual that describes and explains each part of the instrument.

SECTION 1 **Reflection and Mirrors**

Key Ideas

◆ Light that strikes an object can be reflected, absorbed, or transmitted. You can see objects because light bounces, or reflects, off them.

◆ A plane mirror produces an image that is right-side up and the same size as the object.

◆ Concave mirrors can form either virtual images or real images. Images formed by convex mirrors are always virtual.

Key Terms

opaque   plane mirror
transparent   virtual image
translucent   concave mirror
ray   focal point
regular reflection real image
diffuse reflection convex mirror
image

 SECTION 2 **Refraction and Lenses**

Key Ideas

◆ When light rays hit the surface of a medium at an angle, the change in speed causes them to bend, or change direction.

◆ The type of image formed by a convex lens depends on the position of the object in relation to the focal point.

◆ Concave lenses produce only virtual images.

Key Terms

index of refraction   lens   concave lens
mirage   convex lens

 SECTION 3 **Color**

Key Ideas

◆ You see an object as the color of the light it reflects. The primary colors of light are red, green, and blue.

◆ As pigments are added together, fewer colors of light are reflected and more are absorbed.

Key Terms

primary color   complementary color
secondary color   pigment

 SECTION 4 **Seeing Light**

INTEGRATING LIFE SCIENCE

Key Ideas

◆ You see objects because of a series of steps that involve the structures of the eye and the brain.

◆ Convex lenses can be used to correct farsightedness. Concave lenses can be used to correct nearsightedness.

Key Terms

cornea   retina   optic nerve
iris   rod   nearsighted
pupil   cone   farsighted

SECTION 5 **Using Light**

Key Ideas

◆ A telescope uses lenses or mirrors to gather large amounts of light.

◆ A microscope uses a combination of lenses to produce and magnify an image.

◆ When you press the button of a camera to take a photograph, you briefly open the shutter, allowing light to hit the film.

◆ A laser beam consists of waves that all have the same wavelength, and therefore the same color. The waves are coherent, or in step.

Key Terms

telescope
refracting telescope
objective lens
eyepiece lens
reflecting telescope
microscope
camera
laser
hologram
optical fiber
total internal reflection

 **USING THE INTERNET** ACTIVITY

www.science-explorer.phschool.com

Chapter 4 ◆ **143**

Reviewing Content

 For more review of key concepts, see the Interactive Student Tutorial CD-ROM.

Multiple Choice

Choose the letter of the best answer.

1. A substance that does not transmit light is
   a. translucent.
   b. opaque.
   c. transparent.
   d. polarized.

2. The scattering of light off an uneven surface is called
   a. regular reflection.
   b. refraction.
   c. diffuse reflection.
   d. total internal reflection.

3. A convex lens can form
   a. either a real image or a virtual image.
   b. a virtual image.
   c. a real image.
   d. a reflection.

4. The colored part of the eye is the
   a. retina.
   b. cornea.
   c. iris.
   d. pupil.

5. A laser produces light that
   a. has many colors.
   b. spreads out in many directions.
   c. is incoherent.
   d. is coherent.

True or False

If the statement is true, write true. If it is false, change the underlined word or words to make the statement true.

6. An image that only seems to be where it is seen is a <u>real</u> image.

7. A lens that is thinner in the middle than at the edges is a <u>concave</u> lens.

8. Under green light a red object appears <u>blue</u>.

9. <u>Farsightedness</u> can be corrected by a convex lens.

10. <u>Holograms</u> are long, thin strands of glass or plastic that can carry light for long distances.

Checking Concepts

11. Describe the differences and similarities between real and virtual images. How can each type of image be formed?

12. Explain how mirages form.

13. Why do you see the petals of a rose as red and the leaves as green?

14. How is the index of refraction of a substance related to the speed of light in the substance?

15. Explain how a camera works.

16. **Writing to Learn** You have been asked to nominate an optical instrument for an award. Choose the instrument that you think has played the most significant role in society. Write a nomination speech that describes several reasons for your choice.

Thinking Visually

17. **Compare/Contrast Table** Copy the tables about types of mirrors and lenses onto a sheet of paper. Then fill in the empty spaces and add a title to each table. (For more on compare/contrast tables, see the Skills Handbook.)

Type of Mirror	How It Affects Light	Type of Image Formed
Plane	Reflects	a. _?_
b. _?_	c. _?_	Real or virtual
Convex	Reflects	d. _?_

Type of Lens	How It Affects Light	Type of Image Formed
Convex	e. _?_	f. _?_
g. _?_	h. _?_	Virtual

Applying Skills

Use the diagram to answer Questions 18–20.

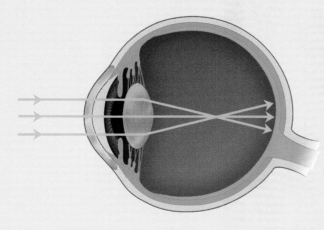

18. **Classifying** Which type of vision problem does this eye have?
19. **Problem Solving** What type of lens can correct this vision problem?
20. **Communicating** Copy the diagram into your notebook. Add a correcting lens to your diagram and show how the lens makes the image focus on the retina.

Thinking Critically

21. **Applying Concepts** Can a plane mirror ever produce a real image? Explain.
22. **Comparing and Contrasting** How is mixing colors of light different from mixing pigments?
23. **Relating Cause and Effect** Explain why you can only see shades of gray in dim light.
24. **Comparing and Contrasting** How is a microscope similar to a refracting telescope? How is it different?
25. **Problem Solving** A telescope produces a real, upside down image. If you want to see a boat that is far out to sea, how could you modify your telescope so the boat appears right-side up?
26. **Making Generalizations** Explain why laser light can never be white.

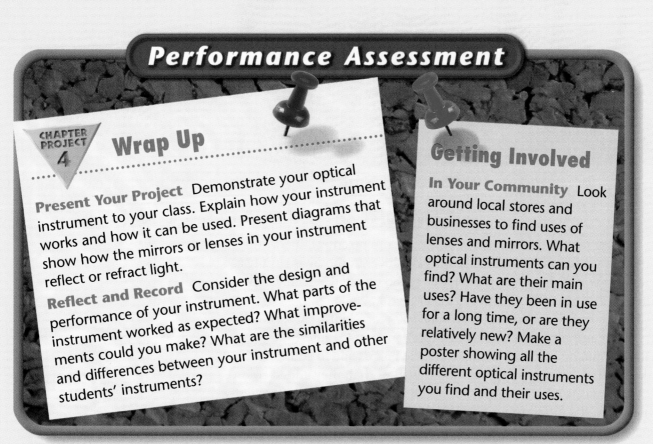

Performance Assessment

CHAPTER PROJECT 4 Wrap Up

Present Your Project Demonstrate your optical instrument to your class. Explain how your instrument works and how it can be used. Present diagrams that show how the mirrors or lenses in your instrument reflect or refract light.

Reflect and Record Consider the design and performance of your instrument. What parts of the performance of your instrument worked as expected? What improvements could you make? What are the similarities and differences between your instrument and other students' instruments?

Getting Involved

In Your Community Look around local stores and businesses to find uses of lenses and mirrors. What optical instruments can you find? What are their main uses? Have they been in use for a long time, or are they relatively new? Make a poster showing all the different optical instruments you find and their uses.

THE MAGIC OF THE MOVIES

LIGHTS! CAMERA! ACTION!

• A dinosaur, 12 feet tall, roars from the forest.

• An alien spaceship lands in Washington, D.C.

• A pig calls out orders to a herd of sheep.

When you go to the movies, you expect to be entertained. You want a movie to make you laugh or cry or shiver. A movie is simply a series of pictures shown at tremendous speed on a flat screen. Even so, millions of people go to the movies every week.

Movies have been around for about 100 years. Until 1927, movies were silent and filmed in black and white. Then in the late 1920s and 1930s, the movie industry changed. Moviemakers added sound to make the first "talking pictures." Not long after that, they added color.

What makes movies so special? Much of the magic of the movies comes from the different ways in which directors use light, color, special effects, camera angles, editing, and computer wizardry. These techniques help to make a movie scene scary or exciting or romantic.

Picking a Point of View

A screenwriter writes the script or story for a movie from a certain point of view. For example, when a movie tells a story from the point of view of one main character, the audience shares that character's thoughts and feelings. The person may tell parts of the story as a "voice-over." If you were the main character telling the story, you might say, "As my wagon reached the top of the hill, I saw the beautiful sunrise." In contrast, the voice-over sometimes is given by a narrator that you don't see in the movie. The narrator tells the same story, but from a different point of view. For example, the narrator might describe the scene with the wagon saying, "As the wagon reached the top of the hill, the light of the rising sun revealed a tired horse and an even more tired driver."

The movie *Babe* begins with a narrator's voice describing what happens to pigs when they leave the farm. Then the camera zooms in on Babe, a pig who has the ability to carry on conversations with his animal friends. The movie alternates between Babe's point of view and the narrator's.

Often, the point of view shifts from character to character as the camera moves. In a hospital scene, for instance, the camera may look up from the patient's point of view. Then the camera may look down at the patient, representing the point of view of doctors, nurses, or family members.

Editing is key to the movemaking process. The film editors, as well as the director, decide what the audience will see in each shot. They also plan actions and conversations that make people like or admire certain characters and dislike others.

These camera operators are filming a movie that takes place in France during the 1830s.

Language Arts Activity

Think of a story or book you have read that you would like to see as a movie. In one or two paragraphs, write a summary of the plot of the movie. Then explain what point of view you would use to tell the story as a movie. Why would you choose that point of view?

How Pictures Seem to Move

The movie opens. The film rolls, and the action begins. What is happening? A movie is a fast-moving series of small photographs projected onto a screen. The pictures appear so fast—at about 24 pictures per second—that your eyes blend them together in continuous motion. But your eyes are tricking you. You are seeing an optical illusion.

When you watch a movie, your eyes see each picture for just a fraction of a second. Then the picture is replaced by the next one. The pictures move so fast that even when one image is gone, your brain continues to see it. Seeing this after-image is called "persistence of vision." It creates the illusion of motion.

Many discoveries and inventions in the 1800s combined to make the first motion picture. For example, in 1834, a toy called a zoetrope was invented. The zoetrope contained pictures inside a drumlike device with slits. People could spin the drum while looking through the slits. The motion of the zoetrope made the pictures appear to move.

By the late 1800s, American inventor Thomas Edison was working on a movie camera. It used a plastic called celluloid to coat film. Edison made the film 35 millimeters wide, a width still used today. Edison punched holes along the edge of the film so it would wind on a spool. If you've loaded film into a camera, you've seen these holes. In the late 1920s, moviemakers added another strip to the film that gave sound to movies.

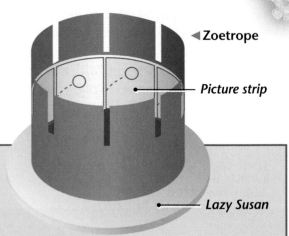

◄ Zoetrope

— Picture strip

— Lazy Susan

Science Activity

Make your own moving picture by building a zoetrope.

◆ Cut a strip of white paper 45.5 cm by 7.5 cm. Mark the strip to make 8 equal picture frames.

◆ Near the center of the first frame, draw a picture. Your picture should be a simple outline of an object such as an animal or person.

◆ Draw your object again in the second frame, but change its position slightly. Repeat the step until you have drawn the object in every frame. Remember to change its position a bit each time, as shown in the illustration below.

◆ Cut a piece of black construction paper to measure 45.5 cm by 15 cm.

◆ Mark 8 vertical slits on the top half of the black paper, each 5.5 cm apart. Cut the slits, making each 4 mm wide and 7.5 cm deep.

◆ Tape the black paper into a circle with the slits on top.

◆ Tape the picture strip into a circle with the pictures on the inside. Slide the strip inside the black circle to create your zoetrope.

◆ Place your zoetrope on a record player or lazy Susan. Center it. Look through the slits as you spin the zoetrope. What do you see?

Model makers built a number of small-scale ship models to use in the movie *TITANIC*®.

Making Models

A sinking luxury liner, a fiery train crash, a city devastated by an earthquake—these scenes look real on the screen. But moviemakers don't sink ships or destroy cities. They use models.

Often a movie uses several models in different sizes. The makers of the movie *TITANIC*, for example, built a nearly full-size model of one side of the huge ship. It floated in a tank big enough to hold 65 million liters of water. Another large tank held full-size models of different rooms and decks on the ship. These models were used for scenes with actors.

The movie also used smaller *Titanic* models that were built to scale. Scale is a ratio that compares the measurements of a model to the actual size of the object. One *Titanic* model was built to a scale of 1 : 20 (1 meter in the model to 20 meters in actual size). Even so, it was still almost 14 meters long. Interior curtains and furniture were added to make the model look real. After scenes were filmed with this model, computer-generated images added water, smoke curling from smokestacks, and passengers.

Models must be to scale. For example, if a car is 3.5 meters (350 centimeters) long, a model at a scale of 1 : 16 would be almost 22 centimeters long. A larger model of the car, at 1 : 4, would be about 87.5 centimeters long.

Camera tricks make models look more real. Because miniatures weigh less than actual objects, they move differently. Instead of crashing through a wall, a model car might bounce off it. To solve this problem, directors often photograph miniatures moving slowly. This makes the models appear to move like larger, heavier objects. Other camera tricks can make a tiny model look larger and farther away.

Math Activity

Sketch a simple scene, such as a room interior or a city scene. Pick four objects in the scene and estimate or measure the actual size of each. The objects could include a chair, a person, a car, or a skyscraper. (*Note:* One story in a modern building equals about 4 meters.) Decide on a scale for your model, such as 1 : 4, 1 : 12, or 1 : 16. After determining the actual sizes of the objects, calculate the size of each scale model.

A Trip to the Moon, 1902
This early French movie represents an astronomer's dream. In the dream, men travel to the moon inside a capsule shot from a giant cannon.

Them!, 1954
In this 1954 movie, nuclear tests in the American southwest create mutant giant ants.

Reflecting the Times

When moviemakers look for an idea for a new movie, they think first about what people are interested in seeing. Moviemakers want to know what's important to people. Advances in science and technology and recent events in history all influence people. Movies often reflect changes in people's lives.

In the early 1900s, people were just beginning to fly airplanes. Early science fiction movies of the 1920s and 1930s were pure fantasy.

By the 1950s, space flight technology was developing. In 1957, the Soviet Union sent the first satellite, *Sputnik,* into orbit. Soon after, the United States and the Soviet Union were competing in space exploration. Both nations also were making powerful nuclear weapons. The idea of nuclear war frightened people. Many movies of the 1950s and 1960s reflected these fears. Giant insects and other monsters appeared on movie screens. Science fiction movies featured alien invasions.

The "space race" continued in the 1960s. American astronauts and Russian cosmonauts orbited Earth. In July 1969, three American astronauts became the first people to reach the moon. Later, space probes sent back pictures of other planets. These space flights made people dream about space travel. About the same time, people began using computers. Some people were afraid the new machines would control them. In the 1968 movie *2001: A Space Odyssey,* the computer HAL did just that.

Interest in space kept science fiction movies popular in the 1980s and 1990s. By that time, computers were part of everyday life. They were

E. T., 1982

E. T. is an alien stranded on Earth. He is found by a 10-year-old boy, and they become friends.

not instruments to be feared. Tension between the United States and Russia was relaxing. Movies seemed more optimistic about the future than in the 1950s. In popular movies such as *E.T.* and *Close Encounters of the Third Kind*, the human characters showed more curiosity than fear about aliens—even those that visited Earth. The movie *Men in Black* featured aliens who were more often humorous than threatening.

Social Studies Activity

Think of some recent movies that you and others may have seen. With your classmates, organize a panel discussion on the links between movies and current events. Think about the changes that have occurred in the world around you. How have space probes, planet explorations, computers, video games, the Internet, and political events influenced these movies?

Tie It Together

Making a Movie

Put your movie ideas into action. With your classmates, plan a short (10–15 minute) movie. If possible, use a video camera to make your movie. Use what you've learned about point of view, the use of scale models, and editing.

◆ Think of a subject or event for your movie. As a class, outline the script for the movie.

◆ Work in small groups to make storyboards—drawings showing key scenes in the movie.

◆ Choose a director, actors, a camera operator, and a film editor.

◆ Assign groups to plan lights, sound effects, model-building, props, background painting, and photography.

◆ After shooting and editing your movie, present it for other students in your school.

Think Like a Scientist

Although you may not know it, you think like a scientist every day. Whenever you ask a question and explore possible answers, you use many of the same skills that scientists do. Some of these skills are described on this page.

Observing

When you use one or more of your five senses to gather information about the world, you are **observing.** Hearing a dog bark, counting twelve green seeds, and smelling smoke are all observations. To increase the power of their senses, scientists sometimes use microscopes, telescopes, or other instruments that help them make more detailed observations.

An observation must be factual and accurate—an exact report of what your senses detect. It is important to keep careful records of your observations in science class by writing or drawing in a notebook. The information collected through observations is called evidence, or data.

Inferring

When you explain or interpret an observation, you are **inferring,** or making an inference. For example, if you hear your dog barking, you may infer that someone is at your front door. To make this inference, you combine the evidence—the barking dog—and your experience or knowledge—you know that your dog barks when strangers approach—to reach a logical conclusion.

Notice that an inference is not a fact; it is only one of many possible explanations for an observation. For example, your dog may be barking because it wants to go for a walk. An inference may turn out to be incorrect even if it is based on accurate observations and logical reasoning. The only way to find out if an inference is correct is to investigate further.

Predicting

When you listen to the weather forecast, you hear many predictions about the next day's weather—what the temperature will be, whether it will rain, and how windy it will be. Weather forecasters use observations and knowledge of weather patterns to predict the weather. The skill of **predicting** involves making an inference about a future event based on current evidence or past experience.

Because a prediction is an inference, it may prove to be false. In science class, you can test some of your predictions by doing experiments. For example, suppose you predict that larger paper airplanes can fly farther than smaller airplanes. How could you test your prediction?

 Use the photograph to answer the questions below.

Observing Look closely at the photograph. List at least three observations.

Inferring Use your observations to make an inference about what has happened. What experience or knowledge did you use to make the inference?

Predicting Predict what will happen next. On what evidence or experience do you base your prediction?

Classifying

Could you imagine searching for a book in the library if the books were shelved in no particular order? Your trip to the library would be an all-day event! Luckily, librarians group together books on similar topics or by the same author. Grouping together items that are alike in some way is called **classifying.** You can classify items in many ways: by size, by shape, by use, and by other important characteristics.

Like librarians, scientists use the skill of classifying to organize information and objects. When things are sorted into groups, the relationships among them become easier to understand.

ACTIVITY

Classify the objects in the photograph into two groups based on any characteristic you choose. Then use another characteristic to classify the objects into three groups.

Making Models

Have you ever drawn a picture to help someone understand what you were saying? Such a drawing is one type of model. A model is a picture, diagram, computer image, or other representation of a complex object or process. **Making models** helps people understand things that they cannot observe directly.

Scientists often use models to represent things that are either very large or very small, such as the planets in the solar system, or the parts of a cell. Such models are physical models—drawings or three-dimensional structures that look like the real thing. Other models are mental models—mathematical equations or words that describe how something works.

ACTIVITY

This student is using a model to demonstrate what causes day and night on Earth. What do the flashlight and the tennis ball in the model represent?

Communicating

Whenever you talk on the phone, write a letter, or listen to your teacher at school, you are communicating. **Communicating** is the process of sharing ideas and information with other people. Communicating effectively requires many skills, including writing, reading, speaking, listening, and making models.

Scientists communicate to share results, information, and opinions. Scientists often communicate about their work in journals, over the telephone, in

letters, and on the Internet. They also attend scientific meetings where they share their ideas with one another in person.

ACTIVITY

On a sheet of paper, write out clear, detailed directions for tying your shoe. Then exchange directions with a partner. Follow your partner's directions exactly. How successful were you at tying your shoe? How could your partner have communicated more clearly?

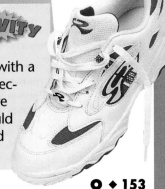

Making Measurements

When scientists make observations, it is not sufficient to say that something is "big" or "heavy." Instead, scientists use instruments to measure just how big or heavy an object is. By measuring, scientists can express their observations more precisely and communicate more information about what they observe.

Measuring in SI

The standard system of measurement used by scientists around the world is known as the International System of Units, which is abbreviated as SI (in French, *Système International d'Unités*). SI units are easy to use because they are based on multiples of 10. Each unit is ten times larger than the next smallest unit and one tenth the size of the next largest unit. The table lists the prefixes used to name the most common SI units.

Common SI Prefixes		
Prefix	**Symbol**	**Meaning**
kilo-	k	1,000
hecto-	h	100
deka-	da	10
deci-	d	0.1 (one tenth)
centi-	c	0.01 (one hundredth)
milli-	m	0.001 (one thousandth)

Length To measure length, or the distance between two points, the unit of measure is the **meter (m).** One meter is the approximate distance from the floor to a doorknob. Long distances, such as the distance between two cities, are measured in kilometers (km). Small lengths are measured in centimeters (cm) or millimeters (mm). Scientists use metric rulers and meter sticks to measure length.

Common Conversions
1 km = 1,000 m
1 m = 100 cm
1 m = 1,000 mm
1 cm = 10 mm

The larger lines on the metric ruler in the picture show centimeter divisions, while the smaller, unnumbered lines show millimeter divisions. How many centimeters long is the shell? How many millimeters long is it?

ACTIVITY

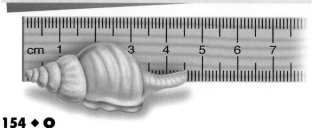

Liquid Volume To measure the volume of a liquid, or the amount of space it takes up, you will use a unit of measure known as the **liter (L).** One liter is the approximate volume of a medium-sized carton of milk. Smaller volumes are measured in milliliters (mL). Scientists use graduated cylinders to measure liquid volume.

Common Conversion
1 L = 1,000 mL

The graduated cylinder in the picture is marked in milliliter divisions. Notice that the water in the cylinder has a curved surface. This curved surface is called the *meniscus*. To measure the volume, you must read the level at the lowest point of the meniscus. What is the volume of water in this graduated cylinder?

ACTIVITY

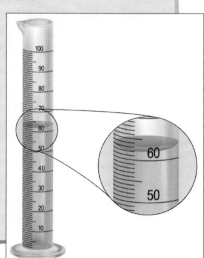

Mass To measure mass, or the amount of matter in an object, you will use a unit of measure known as the **gram (g)**. One gram is approximately the mass of a paper clip. Larger masses are measured in kilograms (kg). Scientists use a balance to find the mass of an object.

Common Conversion

1 kg = 1,000 g

The electronic balance displays the mass of an apple in kilograms. What is the mass of the apple? Suppose a recipe for applesauce called for one kilogram of apples. About how many apples would you need?

ACTIVITY

Temperature
To measure the temperature of a substance, you will use the **Celsius scale**. Temperature is measured in degrees Celsius (°C) using a Celsius thermometer. Water freezes at 0°C and boils at 100°C.

ACTIVITY

What is the temperature of the liquid in degrees Celsius?

Converting SI Units

To use the SI system, you must know how to convert between units. Converting from one unit to another involves the skill of **calculating**, or using mathematical operations. Converting between SI units is similar to converting between dollars and dimes because both systems are based on multiples of ten.

Suppose you want to convert a length of 80 centimeters to meters. Follow these steps to convert between units.

1. Begin by writing down the measurement you want to convert—in this example, 80 centimeters.

2. Write a conversion factor that represents the relationship between the two units you are converting. In this example, the relationship is *1 meter = 100 centimeters*. Write this conversion factor as a fraction, making sure to place the units you are converting from (centimeters, in this example) in the denominator.

3. Multiply the measurement you want to convert by the fraction. When you do this, the units in the first measurement will cancel out with the units in the denominator. Your answer will be in the units you are converting to (meters, in this example).

Example

80 centimeters = ___?___ meters

$$80 \text{ centimeters} \times \frac{1 \text{ meter}}{100 \text{ centimeters}} = \frac{80 \text{ meters}}{100}$$

$$= 0.8 \text{ meters}$$

Convert between the following units.

ACTIVITY

1. 600 millimeters = _?_ meters
2. 0.35 liters = _?_ milliliters
3. 1,050 grams = _?_ kilograms

Conducting a Scientific Investigation

I n some ways, scientists are like detectives, piecing together
clues to learn about a process or event. One way that scientists
gather clues is by carrying out experiments. An experiment tests
an idea in a careful, orderly manner. Although all experiments do
not follow the same steps in the same order, many follow a
pattern similar to the one described here.

Posing Questions

Experiments begin by asking a scientific
question. A scientific question is one that can
be answered by gathering evidence. For
example, the question "Which freezes faster—
fresh water or salt water?" is a scientific
question because you can carry out an
investigation and gather information to
answer the question.

Developing a Hypothesis

The next step is to form a hypothesis. A
hypothesis is a prediction about the outcome of
the experiment. Like all predictions, hypotheses
are based on your observations and previous
knowledge or experience. But, unlike many
predictions, a hypothesis must be something
that can be tested. A properly worded hypothesis
should take the form of an *If . . . then . . .* statement.
For example, a hypothesis might be *"If I add salt
to fresh water, then the water will take longer to
freeze."* A hypothesis worded this way serves as a
rough outline of the experiment you should
perform.

Designing an Experiment

Next you need to plan a way to test your hypothesis. Your plan should be written out as a step-by-step procedure and should describe the observations or measurements you will make.

Two important steps involved in designing an experiment are controlling variables and forming operational definitions.

Controlling Variables In a well-designed experiment, you need to keep all variables the same except for one. A **variable** is any factor that can change in an experiment. The factor that you change is called the **manipulated variable.** In this experiment, the manipulated variable is the amount of salt added to the water. Other factors, such as the amount of water or the starting temperature, are kept constant.

The factor that changes as a result of the manipulated variable is called the responding variable. The **responding variable** is what you measure or observe to obtain your results. In this experiment, the responding variable is how long the water takes to freeze.

An experiment in which all factors except one are kept constant is a **controlled experiment.** Most controlled experiments include a test called the control. In this experiment, Container 3 is the control. Because no salt is added to Container 3, you can compare the results from the other containers to it. Any difference in results must be due to the addition of salt alone.

Forming Operational Definitions
Another important aspect of a well-designed experiment is having clear operational definitions. An **operational definition** is a statement that describes how a particular variable is to be measured or how a term is to be defined. For example, in this experiment, how will you determine if the water has frozen? You might decide to insert a stick in each container at the start of the experiment. Your operational definition of "frozen" would be the time at which the stick can no longer move.

EXPERIMENTAL PROCEDURE

1. Fill 3 containers with 300 milliliters of cold tap water.
2. Add 10 grams of salt to Container 1; stir. Add 20 grams of salt to Container 2; stir. Add no salt to Container 3.
3. Place the 3 containers in a freezer.
4. Check the containers every 15 minutes. Record your observations.

Interpreting Data

The observations and measurements you make in an experiment are called data. At the end of an experiment, you need to analyze the data to look for any patterns or trends. Patterns often become clear if you organize your data in a data table or graph. Then think through what the data reveal. Do they support your hypothesis? Do they point out a flaw in your experiment? Do you need to collect more data?

Drawing Conclusions

A conclusion is a statement that sums up what you have learned from an experiment. When you draw a conclusion, you need to decide whether the data you collected support your hypothesis or not. You may need to repeat an experiment several times before you can draw any conclusions from it. Conclusions often lead you to pose new questions and plan new experiments to answer them.

Is a ball's bounce affected by the height from which it is dropped? Using the steps just described, plan a controlled experiment to investigate this problem. ACTIVITY

Thinking Critically

Has a friend ever asked for your advice about a problem? If so, you may have helped your friend think through the problem in a logical way. Without knowing it, you used critical-thinking skills to help your friend. Critical thinking involves the use of reasoning and logic to solve problems or make decisions. Some critical-thinking skills are described below.

Comparing and Contrasting

When you examine two objects for similarities and differences, you are using the skill of **comparing and contrasting.** Comparing involves identifying similarities, or common characteristics. Contrasting involves identifying differences. Analyzing objects in this way can help you discover details that you might otherwise overlook.

Compare and contrast the two animals in the photo. First list all the similarities that you see. Then list all the differences.

ACTIVITY

Applying Concepts

When you use your knowledge about one situation to make sense of a similar situation, you are using the skill of **applying concepts.** Being able to transfer your knowledge from one situation to another shows that you truly understand a concept. You may use this skill in answering test questions that present different problems from the ones you've reviewed in class.

You have just learned that water takes longer to freeze when other substances are mixed into it. Use this knowledge to explain why people need a substance called antifreeze in their car's radiator in the winter.

ACTIVITY

Interpreting Illustrations

Diagrams, photographs, and maps are included in textbooks to help clarify what you read. These illustrations show processes, places, and ideas in a visual manner. The skill called **interpreting illustrations** can help you learn from these visual elements. To understand an illustration, take the time to study the illustration along with all the written information that accompanies it. Captions identify the key concepts shown in the illustration. Labels point out the important parts of a diagram or map, while keys identify the symbols used in a map.

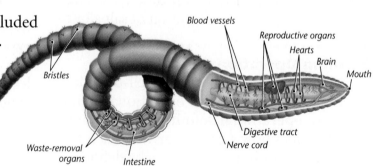

Blood vessels
Reproductive organs
Hearts
Brain
Mouth
Bristles
Digestive tract
Nerve cord
Waste-removal organs
Intestine

▲ **Internal anatomy of an earthworm**

Study the diagram above. Then write a short paragraph explaining what you have learned.

Relating Cause and Effect

If one event causes another event to occur, the two events are said to have a cause-and-effect relationship. When you determine that such a relationship exists between two events, you use a skill called **relating cause and effect.** For example, if you notice an itchy, red bump on your skin, you might infer that a mosquito bit you. The mosquito bite is the cause, and the bump is the effect.

It is important to note that two events do not necessarily have a cause-and-effect relationship just because they occur together. Scientists carry out experiments or use past experience to determine whether a cause-and-effect relationship exists.

ACTIVITY You are on a camping trip and your flashlight has stopped working. List some possible causes for the flashlight malfunction. How could you determine which cause-and-effect relationship has left you in the dark?

Making Generalizations

When you draw a conclusion about an entire group based on information about only some of the group's members, you are using a skill called **making generalizations.** For a generalization to be valid, the sample you choose must be large enough and representative of the entire group. You might, for example, put this skill to work at a farm stand if you see a sign that says, "Sample some grapes before you buy." If you sample a few sweet grapes, you may conclude that all the grapes are sweet—and purchase a large bunch.

ACTIVITY A team of scientists needs to determine whether the water in a large reservoir is safe to drink. How could they use the skill of making generalizations to help them? What should they do?

Making Judgments

When you evaluate something to decide whether it is good or bad, or right or wrong, you are using a skill called **making judgments.** For example, you make judgments when you decide to eat healthful foods or to pick up litter in a park. Before you make a judgment, you need to think through the pros and cons of a situation, and identify the values or standards that you hold.

ACTIVITY Should children and teens be required to wear helmets when bicycling? Explain why you feel the way you do.

Problem Solving

When you use critical-thinking skills to resolve an issue or decide on a course of action, you are using a skill called **problem solving.** Some problems, such as how to convert a fraction into a decimal, are straightforward. Other problems, such as figuring out why your computer has stopped working, are complex. Some complex problems can be solved using the trial and error method—try out one solution first, and if that doesn't work, try another. Other useful problem-solving strategies include making models and brainstorming possible solutions with a partner.

Organizing Information

As you read this textbook, how can you make sense of all the information it contains? Some useful tools to help you organize information are shown on this page. These tools are called *graphic organizers* because they give you a visual picture of a topic, showing at a glance how key concepts are related.

Concept Maps

Concept maps are useful tools for organizing information on broad topics. A concept map begins with a general concept and shows how it can be broken down into more specific concepts. In that way, relationships between concepts become easier to understand.

A concept map is constructed by placing concept words (usually nouns) in ovals and connecting them with linking words. Often, the most general concept word is placed at the top, and the words become more specific as you move downward. Often the linking words, which are written on a line extending between two ovals, describe the relationship between the two concepts they connect. If you follow any string of concepts and linking words down the map, it should read like a sentence.

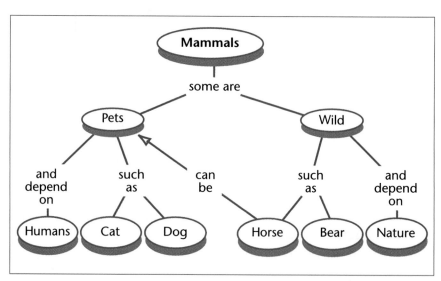

Some concept maps include linking words that connect a concept on one branch of the map to a concept on another branch. These linking words, called cross-linkages, show more complex interrelationships among concepts.

Compare/Contrast Tables

Compare/contrast tables are useful tools for sorting out the similarities and differences between two or more items. A table provides an organized framework in which to compare items based on specific characteristics that you identify.

To create a compare/contrast table, list the items to be compared across the top of a table. Then list the characteristics that will form the basis of your comparison in the left-hand column. Complete the table by filling in information about each characteristic, first for one item and then for the other.

Characteristic	Baseball	Basketball
Number of Players	9	5
Playing Field	Baseball diamond	Basketball court
Equipment	Bat, baseball, mitts	Basket, basketball

Venn Diagrams

Another way to show similarities and differences between items is with a Venn diagram. A Venn diagram consists of two or more circles that partially overlap. Each circle represents a particular concept or idea. Common characteristics, or similarities, are written within the area of overlap between the two circles. Unique characteristics, or differences, are written in the parts of the circles outside the area of overlap.

To create a Venn diagram, draw two over-lapping circles. Label the circles with the names of the items being compared. Write the unique characteristics in each circle outside the area of overlap. Then write the shared characteristics within the area of overlap.

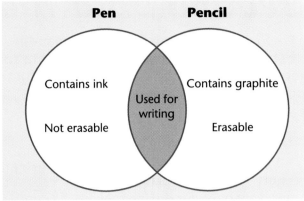

Flowcharts

A flowchart can help you understand the order in which certain events have occurred or should occur. Flowcharts are useful for outlining the stages in a process or the steps in a procedure.

To make a flowchart, write a brief description of each event in a box. Place the first event at the top of the page, followed by the second event, the third event, and so on. Then draw an arrow to connect each event to the one that occurs next.

Preparing Pasta

Boil water → Cook pasta → Drain water → Add sauce

Cycle Diagrams

A cycle diagram can be used to show a sequence of events that is continuous, or cyclical. A continuous sequence does not have an end because, when the final event is over, the first event begins again. Like a flowchart, a cycle diagram can help you understand the order of events.

To create a cycle diagram, write a brief description of each event in a box. Place one event at the top of the page in the center. Then, moving in a clockwise direction around an imaginary circle, write each event in its proper sequence. Draw arrows that connect each event to the one that occurs next, forming a continuous circle.

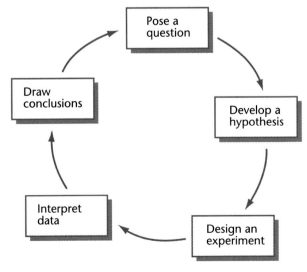

Steps in a Science Experiment

Creating Data Tables and Graphs

How can you make sense of the data in a science experiment? The first step is to organize the data to help you understand them. Data tables and graphs are helpful tools for organizing data.

Data Tables

You have gathered your materials and set up your experiment. But before you start, you need to plan a way to record what happens during the experiment. By creating a data table, you can record your observations and measurements in an orderly way.

Suppose, for example, that a scientist conducted an experiment to find out how many Calories people of different body masses burn while doing various activities. The data table shows the results.

Notice in this data table that the manipulated variable (body mass) is the heading of one column. The responding variable (for Experiment 1, the number of Calories burned while bicycling) is the heading of the next column. Additional columns were added for related experiments.

CALORIES BURNED IN 30 MINUTES OF ACTIVITY			
Body Mass	Experiment 1 Bicycling	Experiment 2 Playing Basketball	Experiment 3 Watching Television
30 kg	60 Calories	120 Calories	21 Calories
40 kg	77 Calories	164 Calories	27 Calories
50 kg	95 Calories	206 Calories	33 Calories
60 kg	114 Calories	248 Calories	38 Calories

Bar Graphs

To compare how many Calories a person burns doing various activities, you could create a bar graph. A bar graph is used to display data in a number of separate, or distinct, categories. In this example, bicycling, playing basketball, and watching television are three separate categories.

To create a bar graph, follow these steps.
1. On graph paper, draw a horizontal, or *x*-, axis and a vertical, or *y*-, axis.
2. Write the names of the categories to be graphed along the horizontal axis. Include an overall label for the axis as well.
3. Label the vertical axis with the name of the responding variable. Include units of measurement. Then create a scale along the axis by marking off equally spaced numbers that cover the range of the data collected.
4. For each category, draw a solid bar using the scale on the vertical axis to determine the

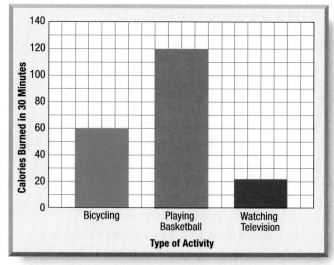

Calories Burned by a 30-kilogram Person in Various Activities

appropriate height. For example, for bicycling, draw the bar as high as the 60 mark on the vertical axis. Make all the bars the same width and leave equal spaces between them.
5. Add a title that describes the graph.

Line Graphs

To see whether a relationship exists between body mass and the number of Calories burned while bicycling, you could create a line graph. A line graph is used to display data that show how one variable (the responding variable) changes in response to another variable (the manipulated variable). You can use a line graph when your manipulated variable is *continuous*, that is, when there are other points between the ones that you tested. In this example, body mass is a continuous variable because there are other body masses between 30 and 40 kilograms (for example, 31 kilograms). Time is another example of a continuous variable.

Line graphs are powerful tools because they allow you to estimate values for conditions that you did not test in the experiment. For example, you can use the line graph to estimate that a 35-kilogram person would burn 68 Calories while bicycling.

To create a line graph, follow these steps.

1. On graph paper, draw a horizontal, or *x*-, axis and a vertical, or *y*-, axis.
2. Label the horizontal axis with the name of the manipulated variable. Label the vertical axis with the name of the responding variable. Include units of measurement.
3. Create a scale on each axis by marking off equally spaced numbers that cover the range of the data collected.
4. Plot a point on the graph for each piece of data. In the line graph above, the dotted lines show how to plot the first data point (30 kilograms and 60 Calories). Draw an imaginary vertical line extending up from the horizontal axis at the 30-kilogram mark. Then draw an imaginary horizontal line extending across from the vertical axis at the 60-Calorie mark. Plot the point where the two lines intersect.

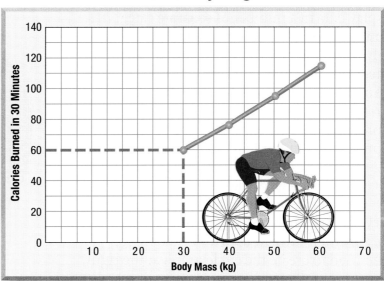

Effect of Body Mass on Calories Burned While Bicycling

5. Connect the plotted points with a solid line. (In some cases, it may be more appropriate to draw a line that shows the general trend of the plotted points. In those cases, some of the points may fall above or below the line.)
6. Add a title that identifies the variables or relationship in the graph.

ACTIVITY

Create line graphs to display the data from Experiment 2 and Experiment 3 in the data table.

ACTIVITY

You read in the newspaper that a total of 4 centimeters of rain fell in your area in June, 2.5 centimeters fell in July, and 1.5 centimeters fell in August. What type of graph would you use to display these data? Use graph paper to create the graph.

Circle Graphs

Like bar graphs, circle graphs can be used to display data in a number of separate categories. Unlike bar graphs, however, circle graphs can only be used when you have data for *all* the categories that make up a given topic. A circle graph is sometimes called a pie chart because it resembles a pie cut into slices. The pie represents the entire topic, while the slices represent the individual categories. The size of a slice indicates what percentage of the whole a particular category makes up.

The data table below shows the results of a survey in which 24 teenagers were asked to identify their favorite sport. The data were then used to create the circle graph at the right.

Sports That Teens Prefer

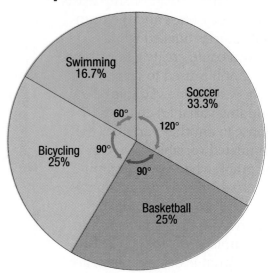

FAVORITE SPORTS

Sport	Number of Students
Soccer	8
Basketball	6
Bicycling	6
Swimming	4

To create a circle graph, follow these steps.

1. Use a compass to draw a circle. Mark the center of the circle with a point. Then draw a line from the center point to the top of the circle.
2. Determine the size of each "slice" by setting up a proportion where x equals the number of degrees in a slice. (NOTE: A circle contains 360 degrees.) For example, to find the number of degrees in the "soccer" slice, set up the following proportion:

$$\frac{\text{students who prefer soccer}}{\text{total number of students}} = \frac{x}{\text{total number of degrees in a circle}}$$

$$\frac{8}{24} = \frac{x}{360}$$

Cross-multiply and solve for x.

$$24x = 8 \times 360$$
$$x = 120$$

The "soccer" slice should contain 120 degrees.

3. Use a protractor to measure the angle of the first slice, using the line you drew to the top of the circle as the 0° line. Draw a line from the center of the circle to the edge for the angle you measured.
4. Continue around the circle by measuring the size of each slice with the protractor. Start measuring from the edge of the previous slice so the wedges do not overlap. When you are done, the entire circle should be filled in.
5. Determine the percentage of the whole circle that each slice represents. To do this, divide the number of degrees in a slice by the total number of degrees in a circle (360), and multiply by 100%. For the "soccer" slice, you can find the percentage as follows:

$$\frac{120}{360} \times 100\% = 33.3\%$$

6. Use a different color to shade in each slice. Label each slice with the name of the category and with the percentage of the whole it represents.
7. Add a title to the circle graph.

In a class of 28 students, 12 students **ACTIVITY** take the bus to school, 10 students walk, and 6 students ride their bicycles. Create a circle graph to display these data.

Laboratory Safety

Safety Symbols

These symbols alert you to possible dangers in the laboratory and remind you to work carefully.

Safety Goggles Always wear safety goggles to protect your eyes in any activity involving chemicals, flames or heating, or the possibility of broken glassware.

Lab Apron Wear a laboratory apron to protect your skin and clothing from damage.

Breakage You are working with materials that may be breakable, such as glass containers, glass tubing, thermometers, or funnels. Handle breakable materials with care. Do not touch broken glassware.

Heat-resistant Gloves Use an oven mitt or other hand protection when handling hot materials. Hot plates, hot glassware, or hot water can cause burns. Do not touch hot objects with your bare hands.

Heating Use a clamp or tongs to pick up hot glassware. Do not touch hot objects with your bare hands.

Sharp Object Pointed-tip scissors, scalpels, knives, needles, pins, or tacks are sharp. They can cut or puncture your skin. Always direct a sharp edge or point away from yourself and others. Use sharp instruments only as instructed.

Electric Shock Avoid the possibility of electric shock. Never use electrical equipment around water, or when the equipment is wet or your hands are wet. Be sure cords are untangled and cannot trip anyone. Disconnect the equipment when it is not in use.

Corrosive Chemical You are working with an acid or another corrosive chemical. Avoid getting it on your skin or clothing, or in your eyes. Do not inhale the vapors. Wash your hands when you are finished with the activity.

Poison Do not let any poisonous chemical come in contact with your skin, and do not inhale its vapors. Wash your hands when you are finished with the activity.

Physical Safety When an experiment involves physical activity, take precautions to avoid injuring yourself or others. Follow instructions from your teacher. Alert your teacher if there is any reason you should not participate in the activity.

Animal Safety Treat live animals with care to avoid harming the animals or yourself. Working with animal parts or preserved animals also may require caution. Wash your hands when you are finished with the activity.

Plant Safety Handle plants in the laboratory or during field work only as directed by your teacher. If you are allergic to certain plants, tell your teacher before doing an activity in which those plants are used. Avoid touching harmful plants such as poison ivy, poison oak, or poison sumac, or plants with thorns. Wash your hands when you are finished with the activity.

Flames You may be working with flames from a lab burner, candle, or matches. Tie back loose hair and clothing. Follow instructions from your teacher about lighting and extinguishing flames.

No Flames Flammable materials may be present. Make sure there are no flames, sparks, or other exposed heat sources present.

Fumes When poisonous or unpleasant vapors may be involved, work in a ventilated area. Avoid inhaling vapors directly. Only test an odor when directed to do so by your teacher, and use a wafting motion to direct the vapor toward your nose.

Disposal Chemicals and other laboratory materials used in the activity must be disposed of safely. Follow the instructions from your teacher.

Hand Washing Wash your hands thoroughly when finished with the activity. Use antibacterial soap and warm water. Lather both sides of your hands and between your fingers. Rinse well.

General Safety Awareness You may see this symbol when none of the symbols described earlier appears. In this case, follow the specific instructions provided. You may also see this symbol when you are asked to develop your own procedure in a lab. Have your teacher approve your plan before you go further.

Science Safety Rules

To prepare yourself to work safely in the laboratory, read over the following safety rules. Then read them a second time. Make sure you understand and follow each rule. Ask your teacher to explain any rules you do not understand.

Dress Code

1. To protect yourself from injuring your eyes, wear safety goggles whenever you work with chemicals, burners, glassware, or any substance that might get into your eyes. If you wear contact lenses, notify your teacher.
2. Wear a lab apron or coat whenever you work with corrosive chemicals or substances that can stain.
3. Tie back long hair to keep it away from any chemicals, flames, or equipment.
4. Remove or tie back any article of clothing or jewelry that can hang down and touch chemicals, flames, or equipment. Roll up or secure long sleeves.
5. Never wear open shoes or sandals.

General Precautions

6. Read all directions for an experiment several times before beginning the activity. Carefully follow all written and oral instructions. If you are in doubt about any part of the experiment, ask your teacher for assistance.
7. Never perform activities that are not assigned or authorized by your teacher. Obtain permission before "experimenting" on your own. Never handle any equipment unless you have specific permission.
8. Never perform lab activities without direct supervision.
9. Never eat or drink in the laboratory.
10. Keep work areas clean and tidy at all times. Bring only notebooks and lab manuals or written lab procedures to the work area. All other items, such as purses and backpacks, should be left in a designated area.
11. Do not engage in horseplay.

First Aid

12. Always report all accidents or injuries to your teacher, no matter how minor. Notify your teacher immediately about any fires.
13. Learn what to do in case of specific accidents, such as getting acid in your eyes or on your skin. (Rinse acids from your body with lots of water.)
14. Be aware of the location of the first-aid kit, but do not use it unless instructed by your teacher. In case of injury, your teacher should administer first aid. Your teacher may also send you to the school nurse or call a physician.
15. Know the location of emergency equipment, such as the fire extinguisher and fire blanket, and know how to use it.
16. Know the location of the nearest telephone and whom to contact in an emergency.

Heating and Fire Safety

17. Never use a heat source, such as a candle, burner, or hot plate, without wearing safety goggles.
18. Never heat anything unless instructed to do so. A chemical that is harmless when cool may be dangerous when heated.
19. Keep all combustible materials away from flames. Never use a flame or spark near a combustible chemical.
20. Never reach across a flame.
21. Before using a laboratory burner, make sure you know proper procedures for lighting and adjusting the burner, as demonstrated by your teacher. Do not touch the burner. It may be hot. And never leave a lighted burner unattended!
22. Chemicals can splash or boil out of a heated test tube. When heating a substance in a test tube, make sure that the mouth of the tube is not pointed at you or anyone else.
23. Never heat a liquid in a closed container. The expanding gases produced may blow the container apart.
24. Before picking up a container that has been heated, hold the back of your hand near it. If you can feel heat on the back of your hand, the container is too hot to handle. Use an oven mitt to pick up a container that has been heated.

Using Chemicals Safely

25. Never mix chemicals "for the fun of it." You might produce a dangerous, possibly explosive substance.

26. Never put your face near the mouth of a container that holds chemicals. Never touch, taste, or smell a chemical unless you are instructed by your teacher to do so. Many chemicals are poisonous.

27. Use only those chemicals needed in the activity. Read and double-check labels on supply bottles before removing any chemicals. Take only as much as you need. Keep all containers closed when chemicals are not being used.

28. Dispose of all chemicals as instructed by your teacher. To avoid contamination, never return chemicals to their original containers. Never simply pour chemicals or other substances into the sink or trash containers.

29. Be extra careful when working with acids or bases. Pour all chemicals over the sink or a container, not over your work surface.

30. If you are instructed to test for odors, use a wafting motion to direct the odors to your nose. Do not inhale the fumes directly from the container.

31. When mixing an acid and water, always pour the water into the container first and then add the acid to the water. Never pour water into an acid.

32. Take extreme care not to spill any material in the laboratory. Wash chemical spills and splashes immediately with plenty of water. Immediately begin rinsing with water any acids that get on your skin or clothing, and notify your teacher of any acid spill at the same time.

Using Glassware Safely

33. Never force glass tubing or thermometers into a rubber stopper or rubber tubing. Have your teacher insert the glass tubing or thermometer if required for an activity.

34. If you are using a laboratory burner, use a wire screen to protect glassware from any flame. Never heat glassware that is not thoroughly dry on the outside.

35. Keep in mind that hot glassware looks cool. Never pick up glassware without first checking to see if it is hot. Use an oven mitt. See rule 24.

36. Never use broken or chipped glassware. If glassware breaks, notify your teacher and dispose of the glassware in the proper broken-glassware container. Never handle broken glass with your bare hands.

37. Never eat or drink from lab glassware.

38. Thoroughly clean glassware before putting it away.

Using Sharp Instruments

39. Handle scalpels or other sharp instruments with extreme care. Never cut material toward you; cut away from you.

40. Immediately notify your teacher if you cut your skin when working in the laboratory.

Animal and Plant Safety

41. Never perform experiments that cause pain, discomfort, or harm to mammals, birds, reptiles, fishes, or amphibians. This rule applies at home as well as in the classroom.

42. Animals should be handled only if absolutely necessary. Your teacher will instruct you as to how to handle each animal species brought into the classroom.

43. If you know that you are allergic to certain plants, molds, or animals, tell your teacher before doing an activity in which these are used.

44. During field work, protect your skin by wearing long pants, long sleeves, socks, and closed shoes. Know how to recognize the poisonous plants and fungi in your area, as well as plants with thorns, and avoid contact with them.

45. Never eat any part of an unidentified plant or fungus.

46. Wash your hands thoroughly after handling animals or the cage containing animals. Wash your hands when you are finished with any activity involving animal parts, plants, or soil.

End-of-Experiment Rules

47. After an experiment has been completed, clean up your work area and return all equipment to its proper place.

48. Dispose of waste materials as instructed by your teacher.

49. Wash your hands after every experiment.

50. Always turn off all burners or hot plates when they are not in use. Unplug hot plates and other electrical equipment. If you used a burner, check that the gas-line valve to the burner is off as well.

Glossary

acoustics The study of how well sounds can be heard in a particular room or hall. (p. 58)

amplitude modulation Method of transmitting radio signals by changing the amplitude of the waves. (p. 97)

amplitude The maximum distance the particles of a medium move away from their rest positions as a wave passes through the medium. (p. 19)

angle of incidence The angle between an incoming wave and an imaginary line drawn perpendicular to the surface of the new medium. (p. 24)

angle of reflection The angle between a reflected wave and an imaginary line drawn perpendicular to the surface of the new medium. (p. 24)

antinode A point of maximum amplitude on a standing wave. (p. 28)

B

beats The regular changes in loudness of a sound when two sounds of different frequencies are played together. (p. 59)

bioluminescence Light produced by organisms as a result of a chemical reaction. (p. 93)

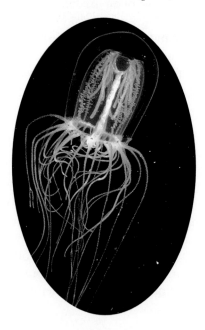

C

camera Optical instrument that uses lenses to focus light and record an image of an object. (p. 135)

cochlea A fluid-filled cavity behind the inner ear. (p. 63)

complementary colors Any two colors that combine to form white light or black pigment. (p. 126)

compression The part of a longitudinal wave where the particles of the medium are close together. (p. 17)

concave lens A lens that is thinner in the center than at the edges. (p. 120)

concave mirror A mirror with a surface that curves inward. (p. 115)

cones Cells on the retina that detect color. (p. 131)

constructive interference The interference that occurs when two waves combine to make a wave with a larger amplitude. (p. 26)

controlled experiment An experiment in which all factors except one are kept constant. (p. 157)

convex lens A lens that is thicker in the center than at the edges. (p. 120)

convex mirror A mirror with a surface that curves outward. (p. 116)

cornea The transparent front surface of the eye. (p. 130)

crest The highest part of a transverse wave. (p. 16)

D

decibel (dB) A unit of measurement of loudness. (p. 47)

density Ratio of the mass of a substance to its volume. (p. 43)

destructive interference The interference that occurs when two waves combine to make a wave with a smaller amplitude. (p. 27)

diffraction The bending of waves around a barrier. (p. 26)

diffuse reflection Reflection that occurs when parallel rays of light hit a rough surface and all reflect at different angles. (p. 113)

dissonance The sound produced when notes that have no musical relationship are played together. (p. 55)

Doppler effect The apparent change in frequency of a sound as the source moves in relation to the listener. (p. 50)

E

ear canal A narrow region leading from the outside of the human ear to the eardrum. (p. 62)

eardrum A small, tightly stretched, drumlike membrane in the ear. (p. 63)

echolocation The use of reflection of sound waves to navigate and to locate prey. (p. 68)

elasticity The ability of a material to bounce back after being disturbed. (p. 43)

electromagnetic radiation The energy transferred by electromagnetic waves. (p. 77)

electromagnetic spectrum The range of electromagnetic waves placed in a certain order. (p. 81)

electromagnetic waves Transverse waves that transfer electric and magnetic energy. (p. 77)

energy The ability to do work. (p. 14)

eyepiece lens A lens that magnifies the image formed by the objective lens. (p. 134)

farsightedness Condition that causes a person to see nearby objects as blurry. (p. 132)

fluorescent lights Lights that glow when an electric current causes ultraviolet waves to strike a coating inside a tube. (p. 91)

focal point The point at which rays of light meet, or appear to meet, after being reflected (or refracted) by a mirror (or a lens). (p. 115)

frequency modulation Method of transmitting radio signals by changing the frequency of the waves. (p. 98)

frequency The number of complete waves that pass a given point in a certain amount of time. (p. 22)

gamma rays Electromagnetic waves with the shortest wavelengths and highest frequencies. (p. 88)

hertz (Hz) Unit of measurement for frequency. (p. 22)

hologram A three-dimensional photograph formed by the interference between two laser beams. (p. 140)

hypothesis A prediction about the outcome of an experiment. (p. 157)

illuminated Words used to describe an object that can be seen because it reflects light. (p. 90)

image A copy of an object formed by reflected or refracted rays of light. (p. 114)

incandescent lights Lights that glow when something inside them gets hot. (p. 90)

index of refraction The amount a ray of light bends when it passes from one medium to another. (p. 118)

infrared rays Electromagnetic waves with higher frequencies and shorter wavelengths than radio waves. (p. 83)

infrasound Sound waves with frequencies below 20 Hz. (p. 48)

intensity The amount of energy per second carried through a unit area by a wave. (p. 46)

interference The interaction between waves that meet. (p. 26)

iris The ring of colored muscle around the pupil of the eye. (p. 130)

larynx Two folds of tissue that make up the human voice box. (p. 41)

laser A device that produces coherent light. (p. 137)

lens A curved piece of glass or other transparent material that is used to refract light. (p. 120)

longitudinal wave A wave that moves the medium parallel to the direction in which the wave travels. (p. 16)

loudness Perception of the intensity of a sound. (p. 47)

luminous Word used to describe an object that can be seen because it emits light. (p. 90)

magnetic resonance imaging (MRI) A process that uses radio waves to form pictures of the inside of the human body. (p. 83)

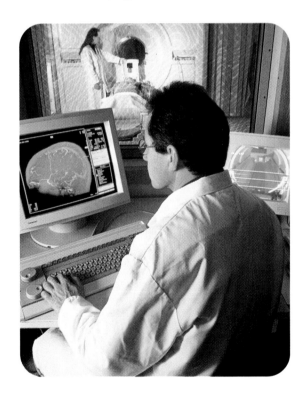

manipulated variable The one factor that a scientist changes during an experiment. (p. 157)

mechanical wave A wave that requires a medium through which to travel. (p. 15)

medium Material through which a wave travels. (p. 15)

microscope Optical instrument that forms enlarged images of tiny objects. (p. 135)

microwaves Radio waves with the shortest wavelengths and the highest frequencies. (p. 81)

middle ear The space behind the eardrum. (p. 63)

mirage An image of a distant object caused by refraction of light as it travels through air of varying temperature. (p. 119)

music A set of tones and overtones combined in ways that are pleasing to the ear. (p. 54)

nearsightedness Condition that causes a person to see distant objects as blurry. (p. 132)

neon lights Glass tubes filled with neon that produce light. (p. 92)

node A point of zero amplitude on a standing wave. (p. 28)

noise A mixture of sound waves with no pleasing timbre and no identifiable pitch. (p. 55)

objective lens Lens that gathers light from an object and forms a real image. (p. 134)

opaque A material that reflects or absorbs all light that strikes it. (p. 112)

operational definition A statement that describes how a particular variable is to be measured or a term is to be defined. (p. 157)

optical fiber Long, thin strand of glass or plastic that can carry light for long distances without allowing the light to fade out. (p. 140)

optic nerve Short, thick nerve that carries signals from the eye to the brain. (p. 131)

photoelectric effect The movement of electrons in a substance when light is shined on it. (p. 79)

photon A tiny particle or packet of light energy. (p. 79)

pigment An opaque substance used to color other materials. (p. 126)

pitch Perception of the frequency of a sound. (p. 48)

plane mirror A flat mirror that produces an upright, virtual image the same size as the object. (p. 114)

polarized light Light that vibrates in only one direction. (p. 78)

primary colors Three colors that can be used to make any other color. (p. 125)

primary wave A longitudinal seismic wave. (p. 33)

pupil The hole through which light enters the eye. (p. 130)

radar A system of detecting reflected radio waves. (p. 82)

radio waves Electromagnetic waves with the longest wavelengths and lowest frequencies. (p. 81)

rarefaction The part of a longitudinal wave where the particles of the medium are far apart. (p. 17)

ray Straight line used to represent a light wave. (p. 113)

real image An inverted image formed where rays of light meet. (p. 115)

reflecting telescope Telescope that uses a concave mirror to gather light from distant objects. (p. 134)

reflection The bouncing back of a wave when it hits a surface through which it cannot pass. (p. 24)

refracting telescope Telescope that uses two convex lenses to form images. (p. 134)

refraction The bending of waves as they enter a different medium. (p. 25)

regular reflection Reflection that occurs when parallel rays of light hit a smooth surface and all reflect at the same angle. (p. 113)

resonance The increase in the amplitude of vibration that occurs when external vibrations match the object's natural frequency. (p. 28)

responding variable The factor that changes as a result of changes to the manipulated variable in an experiment. (p. 157)

retina The layer of cells that lines the inside of the eyeball. (p. 131)

rods Cells on the retina that detect dim light. (p. 131)

secondary color Any color produced by combining equal amounts of any two primary colors. (p. 125)

secondary wave A transverse seismic wave. (p. 33)

seismic wave A wave produced by an earthquake. (p. 33)

seismograph Instrument used to detect and measure earthquakes. (p. 34)

sodium vapor lights Bulbs containing solid sodium plus neon and argon gas that produce light. (p. 92)

sonar A system of detecting reflected sound waves. (p. 67)

sonogram An image formed by an ultrasound machine. (p. 69)

sound A disturbance that travels through a medium as a longitudinal wave. (p. 40)

spectroscope An instrument used to view the different colors of light produced by different sources. (p. 90)

standing wave A wave that appears to stand in one place, even though it is really two waves interfering as they pass through each other. (p. 27)

surface wave A wave that occurs at the surface between two mediums. (p. 17)

telescope Optical instrument that forms enlarged images of distant objects. (p. 134)

thermogram An image that shows regions of different temperatures in different colors. (p. 85)

timbre The overall quality of a sound. (p. 53)

total internal reflection Complete reflection of light by the inside surface of a medium. (p. 142)

translucent A material that scatters light as it passes through. (p. 112)

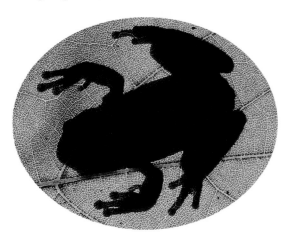

transparent A material that transmits light. (p. 112)

transverse wave A wave that moves the medium in a direction perpendicular to the direction in which the wave travels. (p. 16)

trough The lowest part of a transverse wave. (p. 16)

tsunami Surface wave on the ocean caused by an underwater earthquake. (p. 33)

tungsten-halogen lights Bulbs containing a tungsten filament and a halogen gas that produce light. (p. 93)

ultrasound Sound waves with frequencies above 20,000 Hz. (p. 48)

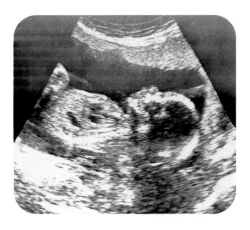

ultraviolet rays Electromagnetic waves with frequencies higher than visible light, but lower than X-rays. (p. 86)

variable Any factor that can change in an experiment. (p. 157)

vibration A repeated back-and-forth or up-and-down motion. (p. 15)

virtual image An upright image formed where rays of light appear to meet or come from. (p. 114)

visible light Electromagnetic waves that are visible to the human eye. (p. 86)

wave A disturbance that transfers energy from place to place. (p. 14)

wavelength The distance between two corresponding parts of a wave. (p. 21)

X-rays Electromagnetic waves with higher frequencies than ultraviolet rays, but shorter than gamma rays. (p. 87)

Acknowledgments

Illustration

Carmella M. Clifford: 63tl
Kathy Dempsey: 20ctr, 30, 45, 60, 94, 122, 128
John Edwards & Associates: 15, 16, 17, 25, 26, 37, 41t, 50, 51, 104, 105, 106
David Fuller: 100br
Andrea Golden: 148
Jared Lee: 42, 62, 76
Martucci Design: 81, 162, 163, 164
Matt Mayerchak: 36, 72, 108, 160, 161
William McAllister: 96
Fran Milner: 130, 131t, 145
Morgan Cain & Associates: 19, 20, 21, 24, 27, 28b, 33, 41ctr, 47, 48, 53, 59, 67, 84-85, 103, 154, 155,
Ortelius Design Inc.: 100tl, bl, 101bl, br, 138, 139
Matthew Pippin: 10, 28-29
Precision Graphics: 77, 90, 97, 98, 101t, 113, 114, 115, 116, 118, 119, 120, 121, 127, 132, 134, 135, 136, 137, 140, 142
Tim Spransy: 66
J/B Woolsey Associates: 63tr, 78, 79, 82, 102, 158,

Photography

Photo Research by - Paula Wehde
Cover image - horn, John Martucci; background, Alfred Pasieka/Science Photo Library/Photo Researchers

Nature of Science
Page 8t, Rob Trubia/Westlight; **8b,** Courtesy of Christine Darden; **9t,** HO/AP/Wide World Photos; **9b,** Uniphoto; **11l,** AP/Wide World Photos; **11r,** Courtesy of Christine Darden.

Chapter 1
Pages 12-13, Jim Pickerell/Folio, Inc.; **14t,** Richard Haynes; **14b,** Rob Gilley/Adventure Photo & Film; **16,** Richard Megna/Fundamental Photographs; **18t,** Richard Haynes; **18b,** Chris Cole/Duomo; **21, 24, 30, 31,** Richard Haynes; **32b,** Lynette Cook/Science Photo Library/Photo Researchers; **34t,** Andrew Ratkino/TSI; **34 inset,** Russell D. Curtis/Photo Researchers; **35,** Chris Cole/Duomo.

Chapter 2
Pages 38-39, Bob Kramer /The Picture Cube; **40,** Richard Haynes; **41,** Russell D. Curtis/Photo Researchers; **43,** Russ Lappa; **44t,** The Granger Collection, NY; **44b,** Eric Risberg/AP Wide World Photos; **45, 46,** Richard Haynes; **48,** Matt Bostick; **49t,** Mark C. Burnett/Stock Boston; **49b,** Martin Bough/Fundamental Photographs; **52t,** Richard Haynes; **52b,** Cosmo Condina/TSI; **54,** Michael Newman/PhotoEdit; **55,** Stanley Rowin/The Picture Cube; **56l,** Spencer Grant/The Picture Cube; **56r,** Nancy Brown/The Stock Market; **56-57,** Peter Saloutos/The Stock Market; **56-57t,** Doug Martin/Photo Researchers; **57r,** PhotoDisc Inc.; **57b,** Index Stock; **58,** David Ball/The Stock Market; **59,** Neil Nissing/ FPG International; **60-61, 62,** Richard Haynes; **64,** Stephen Frisch/Stock Boston; **65,** Michael Newman/PhotoEdit; **67,** Corbis; **68t,** Mitch Reardon/Photo Researchers; **68b,** Francois Gohier/Photo Researchers; **69t,** Merlin D. Tuttle, Bat Conservation International/Photo Researchers; **69b,** Charles Gupton/The Stock Market, **69 inset,** Telegraph Color Library/FPG International; **70 all,** Richard Megna/Fundamental Photographs; **71,** Martin Bough/Fundamental Photographs.

Chapter 3
Pages 74-75, Alex Bartel/Science Photo Library/Photo Researchers; **76, 79t,** Richard Haynes; **79b,** Russ Lappa; **80,** Richard Haynes; **82,** Matthew McVay/TSI; **83l,** Jim Roshan; **83r,** Eric Miller/Liaison International; **83b,** Vecto Verso/Leo de Wys, Inc.; **85,** Alfred Pasieka/Science Photo Library/Photo Researchers; **86t,** Fundamental Photographs; **86b,** Ron Sutherland/Science Photo Library/Photo Researchers; **87,** RNHRD NHS Trust/TSI; **88,** Alfred Pasieka/Science Photo Library/Photo Researchers; **89,** Nordion/Visuals Unlimited; **91,** Bill Horsman/Stock Boston; **92t, 98** Kunio Owaki/The Stock Market; **92b,** Phil Degginger; **93t,** Aneal E. Vohra/Unicorn Stock Photos; **93b,** Charles Seaborn/TSI; **95,** Richard Haynes; **97,** Russ Lappa; **99,** Bruce Forster/TSI; **101,** AP/Wide World Photos; **102,** David Ducros/Science Photo Library/Photo Researchers; **106,** Richard Haynes; **107,** Jim Roshan.

Chapter 4
Pages 110-111, Arthur Gurmankin/Mary Morina/Visuals Unlimited; **112t,** Russ Lappa; **112b,** Andy Levin/Photo Researchers; **113l,** Coco McCoy/Rainbow; **113m,** Michael A. Keller Studios LTD./The Stock Market; **113r,** Skip Moody/Rainbow; **114 both,** Corel Corp.; **115, 116,** PhotoDisc Inc.; **117t,** Richard Haynes; **117b,** Russ Lappa; **118,** Peter A. Simon/The Stock Market; **119t,** John Kieffer/Peter Arnold; **119b,** John M. Dunay IV/Fundamental Photographs; **120 both,** David Parker/Photo Researchers; **121,** Richard Megna/Fundamental Photographs; **122,** Russ Lappa; **123t,** Richard Haynes; **123b,** David Young-Wolff/PhotoEdit; **124tl,** Breck P. Kent; **124b,** Grant Heilman Photography; **125 both,** Michael Dalton/Fundamental Photographs; **126l** Ralph C. Eagle/Photo Researchers; **126 inset,** Jerome Wexler/Photo Researchers; **126r, 127 both,** Russ Lappa; **128,** Richard Haynes; **129,** John Coletti/Stock Boston; **130 both,** L.V. Bergman & Associates; **132,** PhotoDisc Inc.; **133t,** Richard Haynes; **133b,** Camerique, Inc./The Picture Cube; **135t,** Richard T. Nowitz/Photo Researchers; **135b,** Jan Hinsch/Science Photo Library/Photo Researchers; **138t,** Corbis; **138b,** Scala/Art Resource, NY; **139t** Grant Heilman Photography; **139m,** Corbis; **140,** Blair Seitz/Photo Researchers; **141tl,** Jon Goell/The Picture Cube; **141tr,** Bob Daemmrich/Stock Boston; **141ml,** E.R. Degginger; **141m,** Grant Heilman Photography; **141mr,** Spencer Grant/Photo Researchers; **141bl,** E.R. Degginger; **141br,** Will & Deni Mcintyre/Photo Researchers; **143,** Blair Seitz/Photo Researchers.

Interdisciplinary Exploration
Page 146, Everett Collection, Inc.; **147,** Hans W. Silvester/Rapho/Liaison International; **149l,** TITANIC (c) 1997 Twentieth Century Fox Film Corporation and Paramount Pictures Corporation. All rights reserved.; **149r,** Photofest; **150l,** The Kobal Collection; **150r,** Photofest; **150b, 150-151b,** Russ Lappa; **151,** The Kobal Collection.

Skills Handbook
Page 152, Mike Moreland/Photo Network; **153t,** Foodpix; **153m,** Richard Haynes; **153b,** Russ Lappa; **156,** Richard Haynes; **158,** Ron Kimball; **159,** Renee Lynn/Photo Researchers.